PRAISE FOR *THE GENIUS OF AMERICA*

"János Csák has a powerful sense of both present and past. Born in Hungary, he loves both his native land and the land of his admiration, America. In this book he analyzes the problems of America and finds their solution in her principles and her families. Possessing the practical judgment of the statesman and the historical knowledge of the academic, he presents here the fruits of both to insightful effect."

—**LARRY ARNN**, President of Hillsdale College

"After years of assault by the Left, many Americans have either been convinced that America is evil and its decline to be welcomed, or are disgusted by this transformation and question her ability to recover its greatness. While many American thinkers have weighed in on this difficult moment, history has shown that it is often foreign observers, like Alexis de Tocqueville, who share the founding values of our country, and who not only accurately describe the crisis, but remind us of our path toward restoration with even greater fidelity to our Judeo-Christian values. My friend János Csák has written a book, *The Genius of America*, which both describes and addresses the challenges of our generation. It must be added to the list of insightful books written by distant lovers of the American experiment."

—**SENATOR RICK SANTORUM**

"Too few Americans and Europeans understand what makes America exceptional, which has enormous negative implications for geopolitics. János Csák's book is not merely a corrective to that problem, but a tour-de-force that ought to be widely read."

—**KEVIN ROBERTS**, President, The Heritage Foundation

"The title of János Csák's book, 'The Genius of America,' is not only a description of America in its history; it also hints at doubt about its future. For decades America represented hope to millions in the world that the principles of its founding could liberate and enrich the lives of those who arrived on its shores. The Statue of Liberty was not a monument of the past but a beacon shining light towards the future. For many countries, America also provided a model of how society could be better organized to unite, educate, and advance its members. Coming from a different geographical and cultural direction, I resonate especially with the views and emotions expressed in the pages of Csák's short and highly readable book. Like him, I worry about the future of the American experiment, for that is what America is: an experiment testing how human beings unfettered by overemphasis on the past can be freed to develop their fullest potential, work together, and contribute to the common welfare. America grew out of European ideals and became a meta-European super-nation that accommodated but never fully integrated African and Indigenous American minorities. Now, with the influx of large numbers of non-Europeans and the emergence of a multipolar world, the American system is coming under severe stress. Values once thought foundational are hotly debated. Csák discusses thoughtfully the current divisions in American society. The success of America in the past uplifted the Europe from which it sprang. The continuing success of the America experiment this century is a litmus test of our ability, despite our differences, to live in peace and harmony with one another. 'The Genius of America' is not only a description; it expresses a common faith and hope in the ability of America to renew itself, something critical not only for America but for the world."

—**GEORGE YEO**, former Minister for Foreign Affairs, Singapore

"János Csák offers a stimulating Hungarian perspective on America's ideology and evolving values. He discusses the concept of a self-disciplined, forward-looking, and altruistic liberty that evolved as the country grew and its citizens came together in a common cause of making the world a better place, then and for coming generations. He also signals an alarm about a new concept of liberty emerging in the country: an unrestrained individually-oriented material liberty that leads to division, disunity, and a present-oriented narcissist concept of liberty without responsibility—a concept alien to American society until recently. It is a sobering reminder about a way of life that made America unique and successful, and the consequences of the widespread abandonment of it."

—**JAMES HECKMAN**, Nobel laureate; Henry Schultz Distinguished Service Professor in Economics at the University of Chicago

"János Csák is a man of culture, history, and statesmanship. In this book, he shares his love for America as a Hungarian patriot. He sees elements of the United States that are often easy to miss, even for natives. As America and Hungary face similar challenges moving into the 21st century, this book is urgent and important."

—**CHRISTOPHER RUFO**, Senior Fellow, Manhattan Institute; author of *America's Cultural Revolution*

"In these often dark days of the American Republic, even patriots are tempted by despair. Like a good friend who loves you enough to tell you the truth, János Csák pens a love letter to America that glows with admiration and even passion, but that is neither naive nor sentimental about the nation's flaws. As an expatriate living in Hungary, I have had the pleasure of János's intellectual companionship and great good cheer. What a gift he has given to me, and to my fellow American readers, with *The Genius Of America*. May János Csák's wise words summon from the hearts of all American readers what Lincoln called 'the better angels of our nature.'"

—**ROD DREHER**, author of *Live Not By Lies* and *The Benedict Option*

"János Csák casts an admiring Hungarian eye on the genius of America, its roots, and its quirks. The Yanks owned one century, the twentieth, scientifically, culturally, militarily. Will the American genius enable them to own another one?"
—**TIBOR FISCHER**, author of *Under the Frog* and *The Thought Gang*

"Alexis de Tocqueville once wrote, 'The greatness of America lies not in being more enlightened than any other nation, but rather in her ability to repair her faults.' Sigmund Freud had a less optimistic view of this country when he said, 'America is the most grandiose experiment the world has seen, but I am afraid it is not going to be a success.' Fortunately there was also Winston Churchill, who noted, 'Americans will always do the right thing, but only after they have tried everything else.' Clearly, my former student János Csák seems to have taken these comments to heart, making an impressive effort in his *The Genius of America* to understand the intellectual and spiritual underpinnings of the country that is America. Anyone who seeks a deeper understanding of what makes this country 'the land of the free and the home of the brave' would do well to read this very thoughtful book."
—**MANFRED F. R. KETS DE VRIES**, Distinguished Clinical Professor of Leadership Development and Organizational Change, INSEAD; author of *Leading Wisely: Becoming a Reflective Leader in Turbulent Times*

"Like Tocqueville's *Democracy in America* almost 200 years ago, János Csák's *The Genius of America* is an invaluable explanation of America to Europeans and to Americans themselves today. This book needs to be read by every citizen and politician in America as a necessary first step to understanding why we are in the fix we are in and how we get out of it. Hemingway taught us never to write about a place until we are away from it, because that's how we gain perspective. János Csák has lived in America, admires America, and cares for the future of America; this book is an invitation for Americans to re-learn what has been forgotten about their nation's founding principles and the political *creative destruction* that charted American progress for centuries, an invitation more effectively delivered to Americans by a 'visitor'—like Tocqueville in his day—than anyone in the American establishment today."

—**ZOLTAN POZSAR**, Founder and CEO, Ex Uno Plures; former senior adviser to the U.S. Treasury

"American conservatives have been deeply divided in recent years, quarreling incessantly about our past and our future, our principles and our prospects, our virtues and our vices, our liberties and what binds us together. In this slim volume, the strong Hungarian voice of János Csák breaks through the noise of our family feud and shows us a better way to love America, and also, perhaps, a better way of saving it."

—**C. C. PECKNOLD**, Professor of Historical & Systematic Theology, The Catholic University of America; author of *Christianity and Politics*

"In *The Genius of America*, János Csák holds up a parabolic mirror to American history, offering a succinct yet expansive view that only an external observer could provide. The book distills vast historical narratives into essential insights, revealing the American spirit from a unique perspective. Csák's insights serve as a compelling invitation to view American identity through a broader, yet distinctly focused lens, offering revelations as enlightening as they are thought-provoking."

—**ALBERT-LÁSZLÓ BARABÁSI**, Robert Gray Dodge Professor of Network Science at Northeastern University

"*The Genius of America* comes at a pivotal moment in U.S. history to remind us of the principles on which our Founding Fathers based their wildly successful 'American experiment': sovereignty of 'we the people,' freedom, justice, and equality before the law. At times in U.S. history, the self-interest and hypocrisy of men have contradicted these principles, such as during slavery and injustices toward American Indians. In pointing this out, Csák hits upon a crucial lack in current U.S. efforts to ensure its national survival: an understanding that the virtues of our founding are instilled in American citizens by our dearest and most basic institutions—family, church, and education—and that our very survival depends upon their careful nurture."

—**SHEA BRADLEY-FARRELL**, President, Counterpoint Institute; author of *Last Warning to the West*

"For almost two hundred years, the startling fact of America's existence has generated a cottage industry of writers trying to make sense of it and distill its essence, either to understand its exceptionalism or to find what deeper rules may undergird it, regarding the human condition or society itself, from which we can all learn. Csák's contribution to this literature is both fresh and succinct. The essence of this book's originality is in the author's view that the country is best understood as a drama, and that the contradictions and internal conflicts of America are not unfortunate by-products, but essential characteristics of the country's 'genius.' America's dissents with itself are the very engine of its awesome ability to adapt, renew, and overcome. In allowing for competition between its more shallow hubrises, America can perhaps teach us all a deeper form of humility. As such, Csák's book is not only a window on the new world from the perspective of the old, but a mirror the latter can hold up to itself."

—**CALUM T. M. NICHOLSON**, Head of Research at the Climate Policy Institute; lecturer at the Institute of Continuing Education at the University of Cambridge

THE GENIUS OF AMERICA

The
GENIUS
of
AMERICA

JÁNOS ZOLTÁN CSÁK

Translated by Thomas Sneddon
Foreword by Patrick J. Deneen
Afterword by George Friedman

Angelico Press

For information, address:
Angelico Press, Ltd.
169 Monitor St.
Brooklyn, NY 11222
www.angelicopress.com

Ppr 979-8-89280-014-3
Cloth 979-8-89280-015-0
Ebook 979-8-89280-016-7

Book and cover design
by Michael Schrauzer

CONTENTS

FOREWORD *by Patrick J. Deneen* xiii

PREFACE. xxiii

INTRODUCTION. xxv

CHAPTER ONE
The Founding Fathers of the American
    Federation 1

CHAPTER TWO
The Theology of the United States 15

CHAPTER THREE
America's socioeconomic and military
    performance 25

CHAPTER FOUR
The internal contradictions of the American
    moral project 33

CHAPTER FIVE
The problem of reconciling American
    ideals and practice 57

CHAPTER SIX
The American Genius Today 67

EPILOGUE: American alternatives 89

AFTERWORD *by George Friedman* 97

ENDNOTES 111

FOREWORD
Patrick J. Deneen

MERICA HAS BEEN RICHLY
blessed. Its material bounty was recognized by the continent's earliest human
inhabitants, in the first instance by its indigenous
peoples, and subsequently by European settlers. From
arable soil, old-growth forests, vast expanses of land,
and freshwater lakes teeming with wildlife, to two
vast oceans, and the underground minerals and fuels
that would eventually be unearthed, America is a land
that has continued to offer seemingly unending riches
to its population and the wider world. The geographic
features of the continent are implausibly conducive
to human habitation and economic growth, marked
especially by a natural series of water arteries, many
of which feed into the major north-south corridor
of the continent, the great Mississippi. The world's
largest freshwater lakes are connected west to east
from points far inland, ultimately emptying into the
Atlantic where the nation's natural resources can be
further transported domestically to points along the
east coast or overseas. A vast expanse of flat plains
make for a natural "bread basket," while mountains
bounding either side ensure constant sources of fresh
water. Two oceans provide both natural protection
against invasion and a means of transportation; they
encouraged development of a naval system that would
ultimately motivate the creation of the greatest military
power the world had yet seen.

To those natural blessings were added others of a
more providential cast. While the continent was first

settled by hunter-gatherer tribes, in the fullness of time, Europeans who were the heirs both of Christendom and of developments in modern science and technology were to spread across the continent. While it is today a controversial fact, few of those who denounce the European colonization of the American continent would support, much less survive, a return to hunter-gatherer tribal life; nor would they particularly favor its traditional forms, including strict sexual roles. Putting aside the rampant "virtue-signaling" that has become a hallmark of our time, with few exceptions modern Americans remain as enamored and supportive of the advances that were set into play with the European settlement of the American continent as our forebears who once celebrated the legacy of Christopher Columbus.

In the American context (and differently, and with varying success, in the Canadian and Mexican), that settlement not only benefited from the natural bounty and geographic advantages of the continent, but was generously blessed by the importation of the legacy of western philosophy and theology that was adapted and attuned to the particular context of the New World. While we continue to debate today over the exact lineaments of that legacy (and will likely continue to do so until the return of our Savior), most agree that the philosophical and theological tradition that emigrated from Europe to America drew deeply on resources both ancient and modern, classical and "enlightenment," Old and New Testament, and even Catholic (if rarely acknowledged) and Protestant. But all of these resources might have been poorly harnessed but for the miraculous blessing of a most remarkable assembly of gentlemen, the founding generation that included the likes of John Adams, Benjamin Franklin, Thomas Jefferson, James Madison, Alexander Hamilton, and, perhaps most miraculously, among the world's greatest leaders and statesmen, the ineffable George Washington.

All these various blessings have been often and widely recognized, even if today—peculiarly—they are regarded as curses by the intellectual elite who populate the leading institutions of America. It might be that the very plenitude of blessings has blinded us to their near-miraculous presence, leading to that perverse form of self-loathing that is so amply present among America's leadership class.

There is yet one additional, if less obvious blessing that should also be noted, namely, the caliber of overseas observers and commentators who have visited America from its very inception, and which has resulted in a formidable literature and repository of observation and explanation. This steady stream of discerning foreign visitors has permitted not only their own countrymen, but Americans themselves, to see and understand the American experiment more clearly than they might have done without the benefit of "foreign eyes." Looming largest among them, naturally first in esteem and insight, remains Alexis de Tocqueville, the author of "at once the best book ever written on democracy and the best book ever written on America."[1] But even without the inclusion of Tocqueville, the genre of commentary upon America by foreign visitors is hardly lacking in formidable and insightful figures. These include J. Hector St. John de Crèvecoeur, author of *Letters from an American Farmer*; James Bryce, whose *The American Commonwealth* continues to be mined for wisdom about the American political system; Frances Trollope, author of *Domestic Manners of the Americans*; Charles Dickens, who wrote *American Notes* following his celebrated tour of America; and G. K. Chesterton, whose *What I Saw in America* contains the famous and oft-quoted sentence, "America is a nation with the soul of a church."[2] More modern and contemporary visitors, such as V. S. Naipaul, Jean Baudrillard, and Bernard-Henri Lévy, among many others, continue to add to this valuable treasury.

The short book you hold constitutes the most recent contribution to this rich legacy of enriching observations about America by observant visitors, in this instance, by János Zoltán Csák. Mr. Csák is currently the Minister of Culture and Innovation in the government of Hungary since 2022, and previously served as Hungarian ambassador to the United Kingdom from 2011 to 2014, as well having enjoyed a career as a successful businessman and executive. While at first glance the brevity of the book, and its general approach of offering summations of American history, culture, and philosophy, might appear to offer at best a modest contribution to this legacy, this initial impression is deceptive. Csák is a keen student of American history and manners, someone who has both spent considerable time on this continent, and who has read widely about the nation he deeply admires, but which also he gently chides for having often fallen short of its ideals and over whose prospects, as a nation worthy of the admiration he feels toward it, he anxiously frets.

If these main conclusions were the sum of his observations, the book would be nothing more than a learned cliché—and, frankly, one that would echo the commonplace that is today one of the animating assumptions especially of conservatives (but also many progressives in the Obama mold), who hold that America needs only to live up to its ideals to become a quasi-paradisical nation. Csák—who approaches his study of America with the burden and benefit of Hungary's often tragic recent history, in which it has suffered under horrific despotisms, cruel tyranny, lost causes, and improbable rebirths—offers a deeper and more portentous series of challenging observations to his American readers. In this, he is not unlike that figure who towers over all foreign visitors to these shores, Tocqueville, who understood America's most admirable qualities to be inextricably linked with others that would likely condemn it to political self-immolation.

First and foremost, Csák is an unabashed admirer of America, as he declares in this book's first page. His opening sentence states: "I have loved America ever since I was a child." He acknowledges the deep debt of Hungarians to Americans for their stout opposition to the Soviet Union during the Cold War, and recognizes its attractiveness as a second home for a large community of expatriate Hungarian-Americans. Like the Poles and many of those who suffered first under the scourge of Nazism and then Communism, it is natural and fitting that a gentleman of Csák's generation should be so favorably disposed and grateful toward America.

And yet, a page later, he tells a short vignette of a visit to a museum dedicated to a minor historical figure in my home state of Connecticut, in which he raised questions about the fate of the native Americans of that region. To the question as to why the native Americans mostly had "moved away," the museum docent (rather sagely) replied, "they had a different idea of the future." In these two pages the reader finds a distillation of the book's main theme: what makes America especially admirable is inextricably bound up with a tradition that ultimately resulted in some of its greatest failings. The source of Csák's quiet sympathy with the native tribes is unstated but obvious: as a Hungarian, he knows only too well the existential threat to existing cultures by the ambitions of more

xvii

powerful nations. The Indians were to America as the Hungarians were to the Nazis or the Soviets, but the Indians had no America to save them from the decimation of their way of life. While it is difficult, and perhaps impossible, for most Americans to discern this analogy, Csák is sensitive to the deep historical irony, even if he is sufficiently gentle, and enough of a friend to America, not to say it aloud quite so explicitly.

This gentleness otherwise shrouds a series of challenging questions that pervade his short and rewarding book. The book's early chapters focus especially on reasons for admiring "the American genius," with a focus on those features I've already mentioned—the blessings of its geography, its founding philosophy, its political institutions, its theological inheritance, and an ineffable spirit of dynamism, ambition, inventiveness, and openness. But at every turn, Csák notes that these various characteristics that rightly summon admiration also generate grounds for ambivalence. The "American genius" is by turns praiseworthy and worrisome, and Csák is keenly aware of the inextricability of good and evil in ways that can too easily elude patriots and vilifiers alike.

There is perhaps no better example of this two-edged "genius" than Csák's brief discussion of America's theology. Csák rightly notes that America's Christian inheritance was often both a corrective to, and influenced by, its propensity toward individualism, greed, and utilitarianism. It is fair to say that the deepest source of the American "genius" lies in what was often the creative tension between its Christian and Enlightenment inheritances, two streams in which the more "ancient" resources of pre-modern Christianity restrained or leavened the potential excesses of Enlightenment rationalism, individualism, and utilitarianism. Csák notably quotes a passage from John Winthrop's 1645 treatise "On Liberty" in which Winthrop contrasts the classical and Christian conception of liberty—a "moral" liberty oriented only to that which is "good, just, and honest"—with a debased form of liberty to "do as one lists"—that is, the definition of liberty described in the political documents of Hobbes and Locke. This same passage from Winthrop is highlighted by Tocqueville in Volume 1 of *Democracy in America* as a "beautiful definition of liberty," and forming the basis of what he admires in the "township democracy" of New England and informing the essence of civic and political associations that he praises throughout his two volumes.[3] Csák rightly notes that this inheritance was the source of self-restraint in what was otherwise the temptation of limitless license.

Shortly thereafter, Csák discusses another theological strand in the American tradition—"Manifest Destiny." A quasi-theological belief in America's providential status, this strand became dominant, largely replacing Winthrop's more classical view of Christian liberty. Instead, ideals of "Manifest Destiny" advanced belief in limitless progress, unblemished human capacity for good in the contest with evil, and an underlying confidence in human perfectibility. One of the distinct consequences of this overweening confidence has been an often unselfconscious cruelty amid self-congratulation: "the suffering, loss, grief, and pain of those who, from lack of resources or ambition, are unable or unwilling to engage in the opportunities of the age and who are subsumed by history, in our case, under the American flag" (65). Belief in the righteousness of "Manifest Destiny" was no less explicitly "Christian" than the phrases of Winthrop, though the later conception translated theological concepts of eschatology into the political, social, and economic domain.4 Thus, this more distinctively modern mutation of the Christian tradition was folded seamlessly into the Enlightenment inheritance, dissolving the tension that had animated "the American genius," and, as a result, has inevitably generated anxieties about the prospects for that "genius," as America emerged from its ascendancy in the twentieth century into a troubled twenty-first, marked by division, rancor, and evidence of decline.

Csák offers an initial diagnosis of this division that pays apparent homage to conventional "conservative" pieties, but goes on to reveal that neither contemporary party is free of the contamination of Winthrop's understanding of debased liberty. In his concluding chapter, perhaps reflecting some commonplace American conservative arguments, Csák initially offers a conventional division between the malevolent party of the Left—the "Puritan, Jacobin, Marxist, Left-liberal Tradition"—and the more salutary "Biblical, Classical, Liberal-Republican Conservative Worldview." It is puzzling that Csák assigns the "Puritans" to the party of the radical left, while claiming that conservatives are the "Biblical" party, since—extending Winthrop's Puritan understanding of liberty—*both* parties today are, in different ways, dominated by fealty to the debased definition of liberty in which people "do as they list." This apparent mismatch—in which the Puritans are expelled from the Biblical tradition—is substantively corrected by Csák shortly thereafter, as he departs from his initial division between malevolent left and virtuous right, and instead recognizes that the American ruling class is largely homogenous in its materialistic, individualistic, and liberationist ethos. The sources of virtue lie not in this shared liberationist ethos, but in the formative institutions of "family, together with

church and educational institutions" that have historically restrained vicious forms of license not only in
the personal, social, and sexual domains, but also the
economic realm. Csák notes that no party is free of
this debasement: "The short-term, results-oriented
American mindset that prevails today seems to be dominated by matters of wealth creation and distribution.
Conservatives are preoccupied with the free market
and enterprise, while Democrats are preoccupied with
the question of how to distribute wealth more evenly."
Csák, revealingly, here offers a corrective not from the
American tradition as such, but from a classical source:
Socrates, who states that "virtue does not come from
money, but money and all other good things from virtue
to men both in private and in public" (84).

Csák's main point is clear: the "American genius"
was a unique combination of the old and the new,
the classical and the modern, the Christian and the
Enlightenment, which—for as long as they were held
in creative tension, albeit dominated in the most formative arenas of home, community, and church, by the
classical and Christian ideals of genuine liberty—was
deserving of admiration and esteem. Csák's book is not
only a paean, but a gentle lamentation. More, it is an
invitation to learn anew what has largely been forgotten,
and perhaps—in that sense—appeals to a particular
kind of genius, the genius of memory, humility, and
renewal. It is a recognition of the need for a distinctive
form of renewal that is doubtless more clearly seen
today by a visitor from afar than those comfortable if
complacent heirs to a tradition they take for granted,
unable to see what is so obviously right before their
own eyes on this side of a wide ocean.

PREFACE

I HAVE LOVED AMERICA EVER SINCE I was a child. I am fascinated by the American people, made up of individuals from a wide variety of ethnic, cultural, linguistic, and religious backgrounds, and by the dynamic civilization they have created. I have been studying American history for decades, and feel personally affected by it, as it is largely thanks to the United States that Soviet rule in Central Europe came to an end in 1989. In the eyes of Hungarians, America has always been synonymous with hopes of freedom, and over the centuries many of my compatriots have found prosperity in the United States. What is more, many Hungarians, compelled by the storms of history to leave Hungary, found refuge there.

I have also enjoyed a great many personal encounters with America, and have visited the country on business or private trips two or three times a year since 1990. In the course of these trips I have met many Americans, some of whom have become my friends. With our four children, we moved to Chicago in 1996 for my work. Living in Wheaton, we became more familiar with good-natured, suburban America, and while working in the treasury of Ameritech, one of the most dynamic telecommunications companies at the time, I also got an idea of what Americans look like as employees, managers, or even competitors. I studied with CK Prahalad and Dave Ulrich at the University of Michigan Business School in Ann Arbor in 1996, and in 2009–10 I worked as a visiting fellow at The Heritage Foundation in Washington and the Acton Institute in Grand Rapids. I have spent a great deal of time roaming the United States, from big cities to small towns, villages, and rural areas. By translating American works of social science and literature into Hungarian, I tried to immerse myself in American reasoning. As a leader in telecommunications, energy, and finance companies, as Hungarian ambassador to the United Kingdom, and as a private individual traveling the world, I gained broad insights into British, Dutch, German, and Russian mindsets, as well as the cultures of India, Japan, and China.

One cannot live without ideals. The ideals of America—freedom, equality before the law, and justice—represent the greatest potential, and most beautiful ambitions, for human life on earth. There is no conception of life worthy of mankind that is more in line with human nature and potential. Without the intellectual phenomenon and spiritual heritage of the American genius, the world would be worse off. American ideals express the hope that, as members of our communities, we can unleash our talent, enjoy the fruits of our diligence, and, if we are humble and lucky, find meaning in our lives and undertakings.

In addition to the appeal of the American genius itself, what happens in the United States is also important to me as a European. The film of Europe's future is being made in America. For millennia, the script and dramaturgy were written by European thinkers, but just as technological innovations enter the production phase in America much faster than anywhere else in the world, so theories imported from Europe, with all their consequences, become part of social practice in America. I wrote this book because I wanted to understand the intellectual and spiritual underpinnings of this vast country and its unparalleled success, as understanding the drama of the American genius can also map out the global future of transatlantic civilization.

INTRODUCTION

O N A BEAUTIFUL OCTOBER MORN-
ing in 2007 I was in Connecticut, heading
from Boston to New York, and I turned
off the freeway for a coffee. Tired from the previous
day's negotiations and the subsequent long dinner,
I was in need of fresh air, so I headed for Guilford
on the shores of Long Island Bay. The jewel of this
picturesque settlement is the stone house of Rev.
Henry Whitfield, built in 1639. The building is now
a museum, with drawings and maps, depicting formerly
local Indians and settlers, on the ground floor, and
furniture and utensils on the first floor and in the
attic. I have always been interested in the fate of the
Indians, so I struck up a conversation with a museum
employee. "Do Indians still live here?" After a short
pause she said they might, but she couldn't say for
sure. "Where did they go?" "They moved," she replied.
Encouraged by her friendly manner, I asked, "Why
did they move?" Her gaze traveled along the edge of
the gift shop ceiling before she finally said, "They had
a different idea of the future." It made me think, for
I knew that the Indians had by no means disappeared
of their own free will.

I sidestepped the problem by reflecting that history
is always written by the victors, and that no human
society, including that of the Indians, has a spotless
past: all peoples have both caused and suffered injustices. Divergent ideas sometimes lead to conflict, and
we know of three practical ways to resolve them. The
first is friendship and cooperation, when the interested
parties realize that certain foreign ideas are more advan-
tageous, and incorporate them into their way of life,

then go on living side by side. The second is competition: the parties live in one another's vicinity while maintaining their own way of life until one becomes stronger and begins to use its power to force the other to give up its way of life, or simply flee; finally, the third possibility is an open struggle between the parties, until one surrenders or is destroyed. This is how the world works, so it is reasonable to prioritize the well-being and peace of mind of people living today over wrongs committed in the distant past.

Still, the question kept arising in my mind: why did my museum host insist on sanitizing what had happened? Out of ignorance? Or out of self-defense, and an effort to preserve a civilized and tolerant self-image, so as not to have to face the morally unacceptable facts of the past? Over time, I realized that the American view of space and time simply had no place in it for the Indians. The "vision of the future" is the existential essence of American life. In front of you lies infinite space, and whatever corner of the world you were born in or come from, if you have the right outlook you can choose which way to go. Nor are you limited by time: you can leave your past behind, and behave both towards yourself and towards others like a person without a past. You can let yourself be absorbed in space and time. It is up to you, your ideas and your efforts, to carry you to the promised land. And it is your fault if you cannot seize the opportunity.

This unparalleled freedom appears to have reached its limits, however, in the new millennium. Americans are facing the end of a period of unlimited growth and mobility, and are faced instead with weakening social cohesion, deteriorating public security, and the failure of expeditions to spread democracy abroad. The system of subsidiarity between decentralized local government and federal government, which used to function tolerably well, now appears increasingly shaky. The sovereignty of elected legislative and government officials is being constrained by non-elected power and pressure groups, as well as ever more intricate state bureaucracies and business technocracies. The existential anxiety increasingly felt by many Americans, especially those from that backbone of society, the middle class, is being caused by the intrusion of values hostile to a traditional way of life that until recently was taken for granted. Increasingly extreme shifts in government policies, alongside economic instability, are exacerbating that uncertainty. The basis of representative governance, which presupposes that on the one hand citizens trust the government and abide by the rules, and that on the other the government responsibly takes care of the public good, is being called into question.

Despite its admirable material and technical accomplishments, the United States' traditions, identity, achievements and ideas for its future goals and methods, are all the subject of rancorous debate. A cultural struggle beyond the Republican–Democrat political dividing line is raging, and a kind of tribalism is surfacing, as if the United States were being fragmented into tribes, with no sense of belonging beyond their respective zip code. On one side are those who see the American project as an exceptional and positive attempt at a decent system, while on the other are those who see in the same story only the serial abuse of power, oppression, slavery, and a systematic violation of human dignity. In their struggles to win the minds and hearts, and identity, of future generations, the two camps reciprocally accuse one another of falsifying history, and there are even those who seek to silence, exclude, or even eliminate dissenting voices.

The internal division of the US is not a unique phenomenon—we read of similar findings in almost every transatlantic country. Pierre Manent's description of the situation among the French could equally apply to the Americans:

> The French are exhausted, but they are first of all perplexed, lost. Things were not supposed to happen this way.... We had supposedly entered into the final stage of democracy where human rights would reign, ever more rights ever more rigorously observed. We had left behind the age of nations as well as that of religions, and we would henceforth be free individuals moving frictionless over the surface of the planet.... And now we see that religious affiliations and other collective attachments not only survive but return with a particular intensity. Everyone can see and feel this, but how can it be expressed when the only authorized language is that of individual rights? We have become supremely incapable of seeing what is right before our eyes. Meanwhile the ruling class, which is not a political but an ideological class, one that commands not what must be done but what must be said, goes on indefinitely about 'values,' the 'values of the republic,' the 'values of democracy,' the 'values of Europe.' This class has been largely discredited in the eyes of citizens, but it occupies all the positions of institutional responsibility, especially in the media, and nowhere does one find groups or individuals who give the impression of understanding what is happening or of being able to stand up to it. We have no more confidence in those who lead us than in ourselves.... We invite catastrophe.[1]

The exhaustion and confusion of Western persons stems from the fact that everything we have hitherto understood in the Western world as human goods is now being called into question.

It would appear that the spirit which animated America in 1580, 1619, 1776, and 1968 was quite different from that of today. According to George Friedman, the United States is characterized by constant change and even upheaval: "The true story of the United States is how it systematically changes its shape in order to grow," and as it copes with the torments and turmoil caused by cyclical crises it "will deal with the pain and confusion and emerge on the other side stronger and more dynamic."[2] In this work, I am looking for some permanent, enduring intellectual phenomenon and spiritual heritage, for the American genius, as it were. The capacity of a particular national genius to endure is manifested in both ideas and practical action in times of tension and difficulty. There are, of course, extinct geniuses, such as those of the Spartans, Etruscans, or the Mughals of India. However, there are also some, such as the Judeo-Christian genius, which have been able to survive in a changing world while retaining their essence. Although we tend to talk about genius in an embodied, personalized sense, it cannot be defined with absolute precision; indeed, it is difficult even to delineate the carrier. Each national genius is different, but it can be represented in various and overlapping ways by the people and the nation, the political community and the elite, or a particular event or outstanding personality. British historian Paul Johnson, for example, sees the genius of the American people in these enduring traits: "strong, outspoken, intense in their convictions, sometimes wrong-headed but always generous and brave, with a passion for justice no nation has ever matched."[3]

America is an exceptional place in which exceptional personalities strive to create an exceptional political association and socio-economic system in the spirit of exceptional ideals. This is the American attempt to establish a free social order. Actors in this drama include American leaders in religious, political, or business life, coming from different backgrounds but animated by a shared desire for improvement, adventure, power, or profit. But what common denominator unites Sitting Bull, Geronimo, George Armstrong Custer, Puritans and atheists, Louis Armstrong, Martin Luther King Jr., and Bull Connor? How can the wealth and success of the Ford or Mellon families be reconciled with poverty, drug and opioid abuse, and other social anomies? What are the opportunities and responsibilities of modern US presidents who follow in the footsteps of Washington, Jefferson, Lincoln, Kennedy, and Reagan?

My goal is to grasp the essence of the American genius—if only in broad brushstrokes—through an examination of the turning points in American history, and the ideas and actions of the personalities who play a key role in shaping them. To understand the American genius, we need to understand in some depth the history of slavery and the fate of the Indians. I attempt to examine the past centuries of American history, including both America's prosperity and success and its sufferings and humiliations, in a factual and impartial manner. The simultaneity of contentment and resentment, or the contradictions between the highest ideals of state and religion and actual political and social practice, are not uniquely American problems, and many examples of these phenomena can be found throughout history and in every corner of the globe. A commitment to objectivity does not, of course, excuse past injustices and grievances against Indians, Blacks, Hispanics, or indeed Whites. Nor does it alleviate pain, heal wounds, or invalidate pride, satisfaction, or joy in the achievements of one's ancestors. The American genius we are looking for is ultimately not Indian or White, Black or Latino, rich or poor, but a specifically American version of the universal human genius.

In the first chapter, I review the genesis of the American colonial federation, the character of the people who determined its founding, and certain organizational considerations. In the second chapter, I deal with the theology of the United States, including metaphors and ideas that give meaning to coexistence and preserve a particular way of life. In the third chapter, I look at the unparalleled socio-economic performance of the United States over two hundred and fifty years. The fourth chapter examines the internal contradictions of the American moral project, bearing in mind the history of slavery and of Native American nations. The fifth chapter considers the political, moral, and transcendent aspects of contradictions between ideals and practice. In the sixth chapter, I review the current state of the American genius, with reference to competing left–liberal and conservative mindsets, in an effort to discover whether there are ideas that reach beyond these divisions toward common goals. Finally, I look at the possible fate of the ideals that characterize the American genius.

CHAPTER ONE

The Founding Fathers of the American Federation

THE HISTORY OF THE FORMATION of the American lifeworld differs from that of Europe, where countries evolved organically from kingdoms to democracies on the basis of a common origin, language, tradition and culture. In Europe, political communities enjoying political freedom and equality before the law emerged gradually over the course of centuries. In contrast, many of those who come to America, whether of their own volition or fleeing persecution, see freedom and equality before the law as a natural state.

The ambition of the Americans who fought for the establishment of an independent United States in the eighteenth century was to create the most advanced political association in the world, without the burdens and limitations of European history—a social order based upon ordered liberty, and in fundamental congruence with human nature. Its leading figures were well versed in the religious and philosophical traditions of the West, and in the effectiveness of various governance structures. They were familiar with the ancient Athenian conception of the rational, orderly universe, and of human nature. They partook of the religious heritage of Jerusalem, including a conception of mankind as having been created in the image of God; of the goodness of creation; and of ultimate salvation. They had studied the history of the Roman Republic and Empire, which separated religion and secular law.[1] When it came to socio-economics and constitutional philosophy, they relied heavily on the work of Anglo-Scottish Protestant and secular French thinkers of the seventeenth- and eighteenth-century Enlightenment.[2]

According to the classical American conception of natural law, the human person is an intelligent being, comprehends arguments, is capable of thinking logically and consequentially, is free to choose between good and evil, and thus occupies an exceptional place among living things. The Founding Fathers were aware, however, that exceptional ability is also a source of exceptional danger. Persons can learn the laws of nature and place them at their own service, allowing them to protect, but also to destroy, the conditions of human existence; they are able to pass on by their example the virtues needed to maintain political association, education, and nurturing, but are also capable of undermining the community by oppressing others. They would have accepted the principle later formulated by John Stuart Mill, stating that "the only purpose for which power can rightfully be exercised over any member of a civilized community against his will is to prevent harm to others."[3] This conception of the human person has proved acceptable to those who believe in some form of Providence, or profess that mankind was created in the image of God, as well as to those who believe that human existence can be attributed to a special coincidence of nature and that there is no divine guidance, and even to those who have no particular interest in anything other than mundane subsistence and the continuation of the species.

It all began in a sixteenth- and seventeenth-century Europe characterized by religious intolerance, with both Catholics and the growing number of Protestant denominations treating all whose beliefs diverged from their own as heretics. One exception was Transylvania, in the Carpathian Basin, where the freedom and equality of the Catholic, Lutheran, Reformed, and Unitarian religions were enshrined in law in 1568: everyone was free to choose the religion they wished to practice. Queen Elizabeth I of England chose a different solution, following the principle established by the Peace of Augsburg in 1555, and in order to end the turmoil between the state and religious denominations, prescribed uniform Anglican religious practice for her subjects, according to the precept "whose realm, their religion" (cuius regio eius religio). Those who did not want to follow the religion of the ruler were free to leave—with all of their property or fortune. Among the different denominations, the English Puritans who followed Jean Calvin of Geneva first headed for the Netherlands, and then, assisted by corporations established with the approval of James I and Charles I, set out across the Atlantic to establish colonies in New England.

They saw themselves as God's chosen people, and were animated by a desire to make the world a better place. They saw in America the New Canaan, the new land of promise. The spirit and rules of the world of brotherly love (*phil-adelphia*) to be built were eloquently formulated by John Winthrop, a wealthy lawyer and finance professional, on the ship Arbella in 1630:

> *GOD ALMIGHTY in his most holy and wise providence, hath soe disposed of the condition of mankind, as in all times some must be rich, some poore, some high and eminent in power and dignitie; others mean*

*and in submission ... There are two rules whereby we
are to walk one towards another: Justice and Mercy.
By the first of these lawes man as he was enabled soe
withall is commanded to love his neighbour as himself.
Upon this ground stands all the precepts of the mor-
rall lawe, which concernes our dealings with men. To
apply this to the works of mercy; this lawe requires
two things. First that every man afford his help to
another in every want or distresse. Secondly, that he
performe this out of the same affection which makes
him carefull of his owne goods, according to that of
our Savior ... It is by a mutuall consent, through a
speciall overvaluing providence and a more than an
ordinary approbation of the Churches of Christ, to
seeke out a place of cohabitation and Consorteshipp
under a due forme of Government both civill and
ecclesiasticall. In such cases as this, the care of the
publique must oversway all private respects, by which,
not only conscience, but meare civill pollicy, dothe
binde us. For it is a true rule that particular Estates
cannot subsist in the ruin of the publique ... Wee
must beare one anothers burthens. We must not looke
onely on our owne things, but allsoe on the things of
our brethren. Thus stands the cause betweene God
and us. We are entered into Covenant with Him
for this worke. Wee haue taken out a commission.
Wee have professed to enterprise these and those
accounts, upon these and those ends ... but if wee
shall neglect the observation of these articles which
are the ends wee have propounded, and, dissembling
with our God, shall fall to embrace this present world
and prosecute our carnall intentions, seeking greate
things for ourselves and our posterity, the Lord will
surely breake out in wrathe against us; be revenged
of such a [sinful] people and make us knowe the
price of the breache of such a covenant ... For this
end, wee must be knitt together, in this worke, as
one man ... So that if we shall deal falsely with our*

4

God in this work we have undertaken, and so cause
Him to withdraw His present help from us, we shall
be made a story and a by-word through the world.[4]

These seventeenth- and eighteenth-century settlers,
led by men of Winthrop's sort, remarkable for their
merit and breadth of knowledge, established a Christian republican order in America in the name of this
covenant. Alongside the Puritans of New England,
numerous other Protestant denominations established
communities in the New World. These included the
Quakers, who inhabited a vast area of forest (Pennsylvania) donated to William Penn by the King of
England in exchange for the forgiveness of loans from
the Penn family. Another community was created by
Anglican smallholders establishing plantations in the
wilds of Virginia and Carolina. They believed that a
life pleasing to God would also make the world a better
place, and for-profit corporations were found to be the
most effective means of achieving this. However, the
dreamed-of *Theopolis Americana*, the American City
of God, did not come into being. Indeed, the various
Protestant denominations could not even live alongside
one another. Massachusetts exiled the Anabaptists in
1644, and a law was passed in 1656 to expel the Quakers. It further stipulated that any Catholic priest who
ventured back to their colony after his exile was to be
punished with death. But despite their determination
and rigor, they were unable to maintain their closed
communities, and their rules became unenforceable
as the number of new settlers increased. Newcom-
ers to North America hailed from a wide range of
countries, and, unwilling to live under the mutually
contradictory rules of the various denominations, they
preferred to adopt a utilitarian approach. Writing in

1781, the Welsh economist Josiah Tucker doubted whether the Americans could ever form a single nation: "There is nothing in the Genius of the people, the Situation of their Country, or the nature of their different Climates, which tends to countenance such a Proposition.... Every Prognostic that can be formed from a Contemplation of their mutual Antipathies, and clashing Interests, their Difference of Governments, Habitudes, and Manners, plainly indicates, that the Americans will have no Center of Union among them, and Common Interest to pursue, when the Power and Government of England are finally removed."[5]

However, many of the self-sufficient, sophisticated personalities within the American elite saw through these differences, and perceived behind them a common destiny and opportunity. What was more, they were able to inspire and convince the leaders of what were then the Thirteen Colonies to support their ambitious visions. They had at their disposal virtually endless and free natural resources, as the Native Americans were evidently unable to organize collectively or to defend their territories. Thanks to the closed order of European societies, religious and secular wars, and population growth, they could expect a steady supply of immigrants. With the increasingly large-scale slave trade from 1619 onwards, it also became clear to them that they could rely on a virtually inexhaustible supply of African labor. As Benjamin Franklin wrote in 1751,

> Land being thus plenty in America, and so cheap as that a labouring Man, that understands Husbandry, can in a short Time save Money enough to purchase a Piece of new Land sufficient for a Plantation, whereon he may subsist a Family.... But notwithstanding this Increase, so vast is the Territory of North-America, that it will require many Ages to

6

settle it fully; and till it is fully settled, Labour
will never be cheap here, where no Man continues
long a Labourer for others, but gets a Plantation of
his own, no Man continues long a Journeyman to
a Trade, but goes among those new Settlers, and
sets up for himself.[6]

The Founding Fathers were convinced that, on the
basis of these endowments, a political system ensuring
individual freedom, equality before the law, and the
protection of trade and private property could make
the United States a thriving country.

The Founding Fathers felt that the successes of
two centuries, founded on a desire for improvement,
adventure, power, and profit, proved that if they
wanted something they could achieve it, and that the
fruits of their labor should accrue to them rather than
to a despotic British government. They understood
the minds of the colonists, and the British no longer
appeared strong enough to punish or subjugate them.
Nevertheless, at the 1776 Continental Congress in Phil-
adelphia, it was by no means certain that the colonies
would vote for secession from the motherland. Each
colony had three options: to remain loyal subjects of
the crown, to secede from the British and establish
their own independent state, or to unite with the
other colonies in a federal state. Federalists argued
that a federal system of government and law could be
created, a system in which the constituent states would
not have to give up their way of life, traditions and
freedoms in exchange for common benefits, meaning
that British despotism would not be replaced by some
form of American federal despotism.

They sought to injure as few interests as possible,
and to include as many as they could in the independence movement. Relying on ancient Greek and

Roman wisdom, they embraced Aristotle's argument for the middle class:

> In all states therefore there exist three divisions of the state, the very rich, the very poor, and thirdly those who are between the two.... It is manifest that the middle amount of all of the good things of fortune is the best amount to possess. For this degree of wealth is the readiest to obey reason, whereas for a person who is exceedingly beautiful or strong or nobly born or rich, or the opposite— exceedingly poor or weak or of very mean station— it is difficult to follow the bidding of reason; for the former turn more to insolence and grand wicked-ness, and the latter overmuch to malice and petty wickedness, and the motive of all wrongdoing is either insolence or malice.... The result is a state consisting of slaves and masters, not of free men, and of one class envious and another contemptuous of their fellows.... But surely the ideal of the state is to consist as much as possible of persons that are equal and alike, and this similarity is most found in the middle classes; therefore the middle-class state will necessarily be best constituted in respect of those elements of which we say that the state is by nature composed.[7]

The Founding Fathers could count on the middle class, since in Massachusetts, for example, the greater part of the White population belonged to the middle class by 1760, in terms of economic status.[8]

At the same time, the Fathers feared that future elected representatives and officials, who, like the British royal governors and judges, could abuse their positions and interfere in the private lives of citizens. Therefore, rules were created that would protect the sanctity of cit-izens' private affairs (*res privatae*) and reduce to a mini-mum the scope of state or public affairs (*res publicae*). To do this, they had to clarify three crucial issues: equality, justice, and the governance of a free society.

EQUALITY

The Founding Fathers understood, and they did not confuse, the various meanings of equality, distinguishing between equality of endowment, equality of opportunity, equality before the law, and equality of material possessions. Equality before the law and equality of opportunity were seen as needing to be ensured by the community. Inequality in the endowments of nature is still seen by most Americans as something that can only be partially remedied: not everyone is born beautiful, clever, skillful, or hardworking, nor indeed born in the right place and at the right time. Few believe that these differences could be eliminated by disfiguring the beautiful, fooling the wise, or discouraging the diligent. Nature, by and large, is fair: some are ugly but intelligent, others are beautiful fools. Equally prevalent are the clueless rich and the resourceful poor. As regards equality of material goods, most Americans still see a certain degree of wealth inequality as a fact of life, and refuse to allow anyone to collect private goods (through taxation or other ways) and redistribute them as public goods without well-argued reason or dire necessity.

The Founding Fathers saw any attempt at "leveling"—the attainment of actual equality in material goods—as especially perverting. It was firmly believed that material equality would be a threat to freedom, because it could only be achieved through tyrannical despotism, and would not in any case put an end to comparisons of relative status based on envy, self-pity, and wounded pride at any level of society. Alexis de Tocqueville, a French aristocrat who examined the

long-term prospects of the transatlantic democratic project through the American experiment in 1831, pointed
out this incompatibility of freedom and equality:

> There is in fact a manly and legitimate passion for
> equality that spurs all men to wish to be strong and
> esteemed. This passion tends to elevate the lesser
> to the rank of the greater. But one also finds in the
> human heart a depraved taste for equality, which
> impels the weak to want to bring the strong down
> to their level, and which reduces men to preferring
> equality in servitude to inequality in freedom ....
> Furthermore, when citizens are all almost equal, it
> becomes difficult for them to defend their indepen-
> dence against the aggressions of power. As none of
> them is strong enough to fight alone with advan-
> tage, the only guarantee of liberty is for everyone
> to combine forces. But such a combination is not
> always in evidence.[9]

At the same time, thanks to freedom of speech, all
sorts of radically egalitarian ideals were published.
In 1785, for example, Noah Webster, lexicographer
and "Father of American Scholarship and Education,"
argued for the confiscation and redistribution of real
estate: "The great fundamental principle ... by which
alone the freedom of a nation can be rendered permanent, is an equal distribution of property. The reverse
of this, an unequal distribution of lands, has been
the cause of almost all the civil wars that have torn
societies to pieces."[10]

JUSTICE

In order to ensure individual freedom and prosperity,
the Founding Fathers, following the classical natural
law approach, considered it just that all should receive
their just deserts, which is to say, what they had earned.

With regard to fairness in the exchange of private goods, the most important factor was seen as ensuring that both negotiating parties should be in an approximately equal position. It was thought that the exchange would be considered fair if, during the sale and purchase, both parties were free to decide on the value of their product or service on the basis of their own well-understood interests. In the twentieth century, US courts broke up monopolies precisely on the grounds that by exploiting their position of monopolistic dominance, they were forcing their business partners and customers into unfair exchanges.

The determination of state and federal taxes (public revenues) was left to the discretion of elected representatives, not the executive, and it was decided that these should be no more than just enough to cover basic government expenditure. Ensuring the functioning of the state, dire need and equity, were seen as the guiding principles for the fair distribution of the collected taxes. Accordingly, federal tax revenues were limited to interstate communications (roads and mail), defense, and the operation of the judiciary. All other "internal" matters, including law enforcement, education, and health, were the responsibility of states or private businesses and charitable associations (*res privatae*). At the same time, despite their liberal economic approach, the Founding Fathers supported import tariffs to protect the domestic economy and the infant US manufacturing industry. In addition, economic development and the provision of public resources to maintain America's leading technological and scientific position are still key government priorities.

However, the fairness of private exchanges and the distribution of public goods are often compromised, and the courts have been given strong powers to grant redress and sanction wrongdoing. The legal institution of "constitutional review," for example, permits any court in the United States to review even the provisions of the Constitution from a constitutional perspective.[11]

GOVERNANCE OF THE ORDER OF FREEDOM

The Founding Fathers saw it as natural that hierarchy should give rise to differences: there are those who govern, and there are those who obey. They thought in terms of a meritocracy, in which those with enough will, talent, and diligence could rise to positions of authority based on individual merit, rather than merely on the accident of birth. Of course, even in the resultant "natural aristocracy," those with a better education and a more developed network of relationships, because of their family backgrounds, were in a better position. Still, anywhere in the world, successful leadership ultimately depends on aptitude and knowledge, and those who are born into privilege but lack talent and knowledge will sooner or later fail in any position.

Individual states did not wish merely to replace British rule with some more local tyranny, but to create a limited alliance that respected their sovereignty. The Founding Fathers concluded that their principles could best be implemented in practice by a federal government based on the balance of power. They thereby sought to avoid the degeneration that Aristotle warned of as a threat to any political entity:

> Our customary designation for a monarchy that aims at the common advantage is 'kingship'; for a government of more than one yet only a few 'aristocracy' (either because the best men rule or because they rule with a view to what is best for the state and for its members); while when the multitude govern

the state with a view to the common advantage, it is called by the name common to all the forms of constitution, 'constitutional government.' Deviations from the constitutions mentioned are tyranny corresponding to kingship, oligarchy to aristocracy, and democracy to constitutional government; for tyranny is monarchy ruling in the interest of the monarch, oligarchy government in the interest of the rich, democracy government in the interest of the poor, and none of these forms governs with regard to the profit of the community.[12]

The Founding Fathers believed that by having a directly elected head of state, the president, together with a Senate comprising two senators per state, regardless of population, and a House of Representatives representing the sovereignty and participation of the people, they could prevent the government from degenerating. This structure, complemented by the judgements of the courts, consisting of complex approval processes, resulted in a system of mutually counteracting "checks and balances."

The term "federation" is etymologically derived from the word *foedus* (treaty), which is related to the Latin term *fides*: the sovereign parties agree in good faith to decide together on certain matters. In this context, beyond matters specifically and explicitly within the purview of the bicameral Federal Congress (House of Representatives and Senate), which is composed of representatives of the states, and for which the freedom of decision, independence, and jurisdiction of the states were declared in all respects, common issues included declarations of war and peace, foreign affairs, relations with Native American nations, the issuance of money, and the interstate postal and transportation network. Despite the sacrosanct nature of states' sovereignty, there have been ongoing disputes between states and the federal government throughout the nation's journey, and the history of US constitutionality is filled with controversial and sometimes overturned federal provisions. The South Carolina legislature, for example, argued in 1832 "that the several acts and parts of acts of the Congress of the United States, purporting to be laws . . . are unauthorized by the constitution of the United States, and violate the true meaning and intent thereof and are null, void, and no law, nor binding upon this State, its officers or citizens . . . . "[13] Tocqueville interpreted such cases without ambiguity: "when the rights reserved to the several States are deliberately invaded, it is their right and their duty to 'interpose for the purpose of arresting the progress of the evil of usurpation, and to maintain, within their respective limits, the authorities and privileges belonging to them as independent sovereignties."[14]

The federal plan, which promised justice, freedom, and equality before the law, convinced the majority of the colonial representatives. The 1776 Declaration of Independence not only declared the United States' secession from Great Britain, but also made clear the conception of man on which the new order would be based: "We hold these truths to be self-evident, that all men are created equal, that they are endowed by their Creator with certain unalienable Rights, that among these are Life, Liberty and the pursuit of Happiness."[15] The loose alliance thus formed was regulated when the Articles of Confederation were ratified in 1781, while in 1787 the guarantees of individual freedom and equality before the law, their legal enforceability, and the rules governing the exercise of power were enshrined in the Constitution.

CHAPTER TWO

✦

The Theology of the United States

AN ALLIANCE BORN OF THE CREATOR'S PROVIDENCE

THE FOUNDING FATHERS SAW the founding of the United States not as a random or mundane occurrence, but as an exceptional and consecrated historical event. According to John Jay, the first president of the Supreme Court, "The Americans are the first people whom Heaven has favored with an opportunity of deliberating upon, and choosing the forms of government under which they should live. All other constitutions have derived their existence from violence or accidental circumstances."[1] According to Alexander Hamilton, the first secretary of the treasury, "The sacred rights of mankind are not to be rummaged for among old parchments or musty records. They are written, as with a sunbeam, in the whole volume of human nature, by the hand of the divinity itself; and can never be erased or obscured by mortal power."[2] This view is also reflected in the seal of the United States. The three sentences on the seal together express the American mission: the American people, organized from a "multitude into unity" (*e pluribus unum*), shall create a "new order of the ages" (*novus ordo seclorum*), "with the blessing of Providence" (*annuit cœptis*).

15

The city of God, the *Theopolis* envisaged by the pilgrims, did not come into being. At the same time, the biblical and Enlightenment concepts of human equality and freedom did meet in the foundation of the American nation. The Founding Fathers refer to equality and the rights bestowed on them by the Creator in the Declaration of Independence: "All men are created equal...[and] are endowed by their Creator with certain unalienable Rights."[3] The conclusion of the Declaration makes it clear that in their conception, human rights and freedom do not end in atomistic, egoistic, and materialistic individualism: "And for the support of this Declaration, with a firm reliance on the protection of divine Providence, we mutually pledge to each other our Lives, our Fortunes and our sacred Honor."[4] That is, in addition to the mutual goodwill (*benevolentia*) which is obligatory in Judeo-Christian culture, they likewise commit themselves to mutual material and moral support (*beneficentia*) and a willingness to make personal sacrifices for one another.

Western territories beyond the British-designated frontier-line of the Appalachians were now open to the citizens of the newly independent thirteen colonies and more recent immigrants from Europe. The Louisiana Purchase of 1803, by which 828,000 square miles covering an area from the Appalachians almost to the Rocky Mountains were purchased from the French for $15 million, opened up almost unlimited space for Americans to satisfy their desires for individual prosperity and adventure. The Constitution, drafted in the spirit of the Declaration of Independence, was considered to provide a sufficient legal framework for the maintenance of peace and liberty.

However, from the first decades of the nineteenth century, in a country made increasingly diverse through immigration, it became clear that a shared legal system was a necessary but not sufficient condition for a population to become a people, and a country a homeland, and for an American identity to be born. In order to bring desires for individual fulfillment into some common framework, and in addition to references to Providence, some shared, unifying idea was needed. What was the purpose of freedom? Beyond individual growth, what bound them together; what set American society apart from others? As early as 1630, John Winthrop had drawn attention to the threat of egoistic individualism:

> There is a liberty of corrupt nature, which is affected by men and beasts, to do what they list; and this liberty is inconsistent with authority, impatient of all restraint; by this liberty, '*sumus omnes deteriores*'; 'tis the grand enemy of truth and peace, and all the ordinances of God are bent against it. But there is a civil, a moral, a federal liberty, which is the proper end and object of authority; it is a liberty for that only which is just and good; for this liberty you are to stand with the hazard of your very lives.[5]

In his argument, the erudite Winthrop quotes Aristotle, who argues that human association means realizing the common good that is not available to individuals, and does not simply mean occupying the same territory, or "merely feeding in the same place, as it does when applied to cattle."[6]

The system of formal law provides the framework for the development of individual creative energies, but, as Tocqueville points out, "The sovereignty of the states in a sense envelops each citizen and affects every detail of his daily life. It is responsible for safeguarding his property, his liberty, and his life. Its influence on his well-being or misery is never-ending. The sovereignty of the states is sustained by memories, habits, local prejudices, regional and familial self-interest—in short, by all the things that make the patriotic instinct such a powerful force in the heart of man."[7] In the first inaugural address delivered by a US president, on April 30, 1789, George Washington spoke of the legitimizing effect of loyalty and devotion to the homeland and common interests: "The foundation of our national policy will be laid in the pure and immutable principles of private morality, and the preeminence of free government be exemplified by all the attributes which can win the affections of its citizens and command the respect of the world."[8] In his farewell address of September 17, 1796, with seven years of presidential experience behind him, Washington further clarified his statement, and referred to morality and religion as the backbone of loyalty and devotion to the homeland: "Of all the dispositions and habits which lead to political prosperity, religion and morality are indispensable supports . . . these firmest props of the duties of men and citizens . . . . Reason and experience both forbid us to expect that national morality can prevail in exclusion of religious principle."[9] Experiencing this, Tocqueville writes in 1831 that "in America, it was religion that showed the way to enlightenment; it was respect for divine law that showed man the way to freedom . . . . It is the result (and this point of departure should be constantly kept in mind) of two quite distinct elements, which elsewhere have often been at war but in America have somehow been incorporated into one another and marvelously combined. I allude to the spirit of religion and the spirit of liberty."[10] "I believe that it is only by conforming scrupulously to religious morality in great affairs that they can boast of teaching citizens to know it, love it, and respect it in small ones."[11]

Founded on religious morality, America grew rapidly in the early nineteenth century, and proved extremely attractive to Europeans in search of a livelihood. However, the belief of colonial Protestants in a covenant with God, or the sense of consecrated mission held by the Founding Fathers, were already proving too narrow to bring together immigrants of different religions and ethnicities arriving in this expanding country. But was there still a common idea that preserved the spirit of America at the time of its founding, to differentiate it from other countries in the world?

UTILITARIANISM AND THE PERFORMANCE PRINCIPLE

In 1831, Tocqueville felt that a form of secular utilitarianism, albeit one built upon transcendentalist underpinnings, was most characteristic of America:

> It would be difficult to describe the avidity with which the American hurls himself upon the immense prey that fortune offers him.... These people left their original homeland in search of the good life. They left their second homeland in search of a still better one. Almost everywhere they go, they encounter good fortune but not happiness. For them, the desire for wellbeing has become an anxious, burning passion that grows even as it is satisfied. They long ago broke the bonds that attached them to their native soil and have formed no other bonds since. For them, emigration began as a need; today it has become a game of chance, which they love as much for the emotions it stirs as for the profit it brings.[12]

By the nineteenth and twentieth centuries, the dominance of utilitarianism, which combined a desire for profit and adventure, had indeed become the hallmark of American society, differentiating it from all other societies. Max Weber, who otherwise admired American successes of the early twentieth century, pointed out that America had broken away from precisely those moral and religious foundations that George Washington had deemed essential, and was moving toward "mechanical petrification":

> In the field of its highest development, in the United States, the pursuit of wealth, stripped of its religious and ethical meaning, tends to become associated with purely mundane passions, which often actually give it the character of sport. No one knows who will live in this cage in the future, or whether at the end of this tremendous development entirely new prophets will arise, or there will be a great rebirth of old ideas and ideals, or, if neither, mechanized petrification, embellished with a sort of convulsive self-importance. For of the last stage of this cultural development, it might well be truly said: Specialists without spirit, sensualists without heart; this nullity imagines that it has attained a level of civilization never before achieved.[13]

For Americans, from the nineteenth century to the present, success means the rise in consumer spending and elevation to the lifestyle of the middle class. The price of this social mobility, and new lifestyle, was the breaking of past ties and the acceptance of new goals. Tocqueville saw that "What we call love of gain Americans see as praiseworthy industriousness, and they see a certain faintness of heart in what we regard as moderation of desire.... In France we regard simplicity of taste, tranquillity of mores, family spirit, and love of one's birthplace as important guarantees of tranquillity and happiness for the state, but in America nothing seems more prejudicial to society than virtues such as these.... To exchange the pure and quiet

pleasures that even the poor savor in their native land
for the sterile enjoyments of prosperity under foreign
skies; to flee one's ancestral home and the fields in
which one's forebears lie buried; to abandon the dead
and the living alike in order to court fortune—nothing, in their eyes, is more worthy of praise."[14] The
consumption of standardized material goods blurred
differences, and the peculiarities of one's culture of
origin began to appear incidental and exotic. After
1820, the "bargain offered to immigrants was never
obvious, but presumably it was something like: 'leave
your impoverished homeland there, change your culture, work hard, and the fruits of the new economic
system will be at your fingertips. Your lowly fate can
be exchanged for a higher one, there will be more
income, material possessions will accumulate, and the
hopelessness of the Old World will be replaced by the
casual optimism of the New World.... The average
immigrant presumably moved into an ethnically close-
knit neighborhood, worked for a time, then left them
for a middle-class job somewhere else."[15]

MANIFEST DESTINY AND UNIVERSAL EXCEPTIONALISM

Thus, from the nineteenth century on, the missionary consciousness derived from the supernatural
no longer acted as a unifying force, and the principle
of success and utilitarianism was essentially an individual strategy. At the same time, the vicissitudes of
nineteenth-century wars against the British, Mexicans,
and Spaniards brought Anglo-Saxons and newly arrived
immigrant Americans closer together. Mutual trust was
a life-and-death necessity, and required faith in the
meaning of the fight, as well as some sort of consensual
acknowledgment of the interests of the homeland. At

the heart of the new American missionary consciousness was a kind of secular missionary belief in American exceptionalism, which in 1845 John O'Sullivan,
still employing religious language, called "Manifest
Destiny."[16] By the beginning of the twentieth century,
another metaphor portraying the common destiny of
Americans as being literally merged together was enter-
ing common parlance: *The Melting Pot*, originally the
title of Israel Zangwill's 1908 play. The concepts of
Manifest Destiny and the melting pot also fitted the
spirit of change in an era dictated by the bourgeois
and Marxist heirs of the Enlightenment, or, as Hegel
put it: "It is not difficult to see that ours is a birth-
time and a period of transition to a new era. Spirit
has broken with the world it has hitherto inhabited
and imagined, and is of a mind to submerge it in the
past, and in the labor of its own transformation."[17]

Still, no metaphor of American unity has ever been
able to resolve the contradiction between these ideals
and either the sin of slavery or the dispossession of
the Indians. These sins cast as dark a shadow on the
Americans of the nineteenth and twentieth centuries
as they did on the colonists in the seventeenth and
eighteenth centuries. Amendments to the Constitution
only slowly extended the "self-evident" rights of life,
liberty and pursuit of happiness for all to Black and
Indian Americans, who were excluded from the melting
pot until the late twentieth century and had a "manifest destiny" altogether different from that of Whites.

In the twentieth century, the United States began
to play an increasingly active role on the world stage.
Its leaders, entirely unaffected by racial injustice or
the inconsistent application of rights, were motivated
by a spirit of exceptionalism and universalist inter-
ventionism. President Woodrow Wilson argued in

1914 that there was a struggle for good and evil in the world, and that it was America's job to "vindicate the principles of peace and justice in the life of the world as against selfish and autocratic power and to set up amongst the really free and self-governed peoples of the world such a concert of purpose and of action as will henceforth ensure the observance of those principles."[18] It is difficult today to see how Wilson, who was re-elected president in 1916, was able to reconcile the contradiction between the self-evident injustices suffered by disenfranchised Blacks and Indians and his own statements:

> An evident principle runs through the whole program.... It is the principle of justice to all peoples and nationalities, and their right to live on equal terms of liberty and safety with one another, whether they be strong or weak. Unless this principle be made its foundation, no part of the structure of international justice can stand. The people of the United States could act upon no other principle; and to the vindication of this principle they are ready to devote their lives, their honor, and everything that they possess. The moral climax of this, the culminating and final war for human liberty, has come, and they are ready to put their own strength, their own highest purpose, their own integrity and devotion to the test.[19]

It is hard to imagine how Black and Native Americans in the America of that time would have reacted to this obviously self-contradictory, hypocritical speech.

Wilson's words did, however, faithfully reflect contemporary American public thinking. At the time of the US entry into the war, in 1917, a competition was launched to find the clearest expression of what it meant to be an American and what Americans owed their homeland. The competition was won by William Tyler Page for "The American's Creed," which states that America is a land of "freedom, equality, justice, and humanity," and that an American citizen has a "duty to country to love it, to support its Constitution, to obey its laws, to respect its flag, and to defend it against all enemies."[20] This creed, like the covenant with God, Manifest Destiny, and the melting pot, remained incomplete, as Blacks and Indians who fought under the American flag in World War II continued to suffer segregation and disenfranchisement in civilian life.

CHAPTER THREE

❧

America's socioeconomic and military performance

NEVERTHELESS, THE EFFEC-tiveness of the US political system is evidenced by its impressive socio-economic, cultural, and military successes over almost two and a half centuries: violence, misery, and oppression have declined, while women and minorities have steadily gained a greater voice in society. In America, anyone with sufficient ability and determination has access to the best the world has to offer in terms of material and intellectual goods.

The territory of the United States has more than quadrupled since independence, from 865,000 square miles in 1790 to 3.6 million by 2020. According to the Maddison Project, the US population was 10 million in 1820,[1] and grew to 336 million by November 24, 2023.[2] Ten states have populations greater than nine million, while 40 states have populations lower than nine million.

Life expectancy at birth for those over the age of five rose from 55 years in 1850 to 79 by 2020. Between 1973 and 2020, 62.5 million legal abortions were performed. The fertility rate is steadily declining, and since 2010 it has been below the average level of 2.1 children per woman of childbearing age needed to sustain the population: by 2021, it had fallen to 1.66.[3] Forty per cent of children born in 2021 were born out of wedlock. Of these, the proportion of children born out of wedlock among Blacks, Native Americans, and indigenous Alaskans is 68 to 70 per cent, 53 per cent among Hispanics, and 27 per cent among Whites.[4]

Between 1980 and 2021, 37.3 million legal immigrants became LPRs (lawful permanent residents).[5] In addition, the number of illegal aliens or unauthorized immigrants in the country was estimated at 11.4 million in 2018.[6] According to the 2021 census, a total of 44.8 million of the country's 332 million people—nearly 15 per cent of the population—were born outside the United States.[7]

GDP per capita, as measured in 2011 US dollars, rose thirty-fold across the nation's history, from $2,700 in 1820 to $76,400 in 2022,[8] one of the highest in the world. In 2017, 51 per cent of the US population was in the middle-class income category.[9] At the same time, however, in 2020 the United States and Turkey had the highest levels of income inequality (US Gini Coefficient: 0.375) among OECD member states which make up the world's 38 most developed countries.[10] In 2021, 37.9 million Americans comprising 11.6 per cent of the population (15.3 per cent for people under the age of 18) lived below the official poverty line.[11] According to the UN Human Development Index, which measures life expectancy, length of schooling, average educational attainment, and GNI per capita, the US was ranked 21st in the world in 2021.[12]

The United States is the world's largest economic power. Though comprising just four per cent of the world's population, it produces 25 per cent of the world's GDP, amounting to some $25.5 trillion in 2022, according to the World Bank.[13] One crucial factor in

US economic stability is domestic demand: personal consumption accounts for 67.7 per cent of her nominal GDP (Q3 2023).[14] The other factor is self-sufficiency, based upon an abundance of domestic resources: in 2021, US exports made up just 10.9 per cent of GDP, and imports just 14.6 per cent.[15] This means that the country is relatively unaffected by external economic changes.

The economic strength of a country is shown by its outward investment and its attractiveness to inward investment. According to the OECD, the value of US investments abroad in 2021 was $9.7 trillion, while foreign direct investment in the United States was $13.6 trillion, accounting for 23 and 29 per cent respectively of movement of the world's working capital.[16] According to the Economic Complexity Index, which measures the complexity and knowledge background of export-import, the United States ranked tenth out of 137 countries in the world in 2021.[17]

The United States is the world's leading innovation power, with 37 per cent of the world's research and development spending in 2000, and 27 per cent in 2019, going to projects in the United States. About a fifth of US research and development spending is backed by government funding.[18] Overall the US domestic consumer and investor demand, and corresponding institutional system, offer a unique, in-depth, and unprecedented business model and environment for scientific research and innovation.

Confidence in the solvency of a state is shown by the loans—from a domestic perspective: public debt— granted to it. According to OECD 2022 data, the total (domestic and foreign) government debt and other government liabilities of the United States stands at 144 per cent of GDP and continues to grow.[19]

Borrowing in the United States is primarily used to finance the current budget deficit. Overspending is largely due to complacency by policymakers, stemming from the fact that US government securities and the dollar are the safest (anytime liquid) international monetary reserves. As of 2022, the IMF Special Drawing Rights (SDR) basket consists of the US dollar (43.38%), the Euro (29.31%), the Chinese yuan (12.28%), the Japanese yen (7.59%), and the British pound (7.44%),[20] in which the weight of the US dollar accurately mirrors the weight of the United States in the global economy.

According to the OECD, the total US (federal and state) budget deficit in 2021 was 12.1 per cent of GDP.[21] According to the Congressional Budget Office, federal budget revenue stood at $4.9 trillion, and spending at $6.3 trillion in 2022. Spending $4.1 trillion on health and retirement funds alone approaches revenues, in addition to the $475 billion in net interest expenditure. These items are determinations, in other words, compulsory payments based on previous decisions, in which Congressional or Senate members thus have no decision-making power whatsoever. Elected representatives can allocate somewhat more than 25 per cent of total spending in a given budget year: such expenditure, to be financed purely from debt, amounted to approximately $1.7 trillion in 2022. Of this, nearly $750 billion was allocated to fund the military, while the remainder was allocated to education, health, transport, and other social purposes. The share of discretionary expenditures averaged 7.2 per cent of GDP between 2000 and 2019, and 6.6 per cent in 2022.[22]

The United States is the strongest military power in the world. The Nazi and Soviet regimes would not have been brought down had it not been for American military strength, or at least their defeat would have taken much longer. The US spent $750 billion, or 3 per cent of GDP, on military spending in 2022, which is 40 per cent of the world's military expenditure.[23]

The United States is the only power capable of conducting rapid and effective military action anywhere in the world, even in multiple locations in any given time. The country has never been militarily occupied, and no regular foreign forces have entered her territory since the War of 1812. An example of the effectiveness of US forces is the Vietnam War. Forty-seven thousand US soldiers were killed and 304,000 wounded between 1965 and 1972, while on the Vietnamese side an estimated 1.1 million soldiers were killed and 600,000 wounded.[24]

Several indices have been developed to depict the given state of social entities at a point of time in the past, including countries in general.[25] We know of far fewer attempts to assess the future potential of social entities, as this requires an interpretation of a future desired state of affairs, a concept of good human life and unity of order. Such concepts face the ancient questions of "how one ought to live"; "what course of life is best"; "[what is] the right conduct of life"[26] and the nature and proper operation of a unity of order that enables good human life.[27] A project in that direction is the Future Potential Index,[28] which is an attempt to assess the ability and readiness of social entities to preserve a good life for their members and reproduce its way of life in a unity of order through comprehending the ever-evolving world, and controlling its destiny.

According to the Future Potential Index,[29] the United States ranks 27th out of 38 OECD countries in 2022. The index is comprised of 22 indicators to represent the human goods provided by a social entity to its citizens. The 22 indicators are grouped in four fundamental pillars. The first fundamental human good is peace and security, as these are required for persons to be able to take care of themselves and other loved ones, and to plan any future activities. In the absence of security, all energy is devoted towards establishing it, to the detriment of other creative activities. In this, the United States ranks 24th out of 38 countries. The second human good is attachment and belonging, which is essential for a person's healthy physical, mental, and spiritual development. Human persons first meet the meaning of attachment and love, care and devotion, magnanimity and equity, merit, authority and hierarchy in childhood. Persons come to understand as a child what is good and bad, true and false, just and unjust, beautiful and ugly, what is a gift and what is a reciprocal transaction. In the absence of proper childhood development, one will find it difficult to connect with other people, and to belong to communities and organizations later in life. In this, the United States ranks 11th. The third human good is care and generativity, which captures one's freedom as to how to provide oneself and loved ones with physical, mental, and spiritual goods. In this, the United States ranks 24th. Finally, the fourth fundamental human good is health and a sense of balance, without which it is impossible to feel contentment, to acknowledge the success and prosperity of others without envy or resentment. Without a certain level of balance and health, one cannot enjoy peace, prosperity, or attachments. In this, the United States ranks 36th out of the 38 OECD member states.

Overall, the US institutional system provides a unique incentive to endeavor, performance, and value generation, a framework that in turn resulted in an unprecedentedly rapid and sustained growth, and that has created material wealth for vast numbers of people over the past two hundred and fifty years. The elemental power of the American genius is most evident in the fact that the goods it offers are considered by a multitude of people, both within the country and globally, as aspirations and objects of desire.

CHAPTER FOUR

☙

The internal contradictions of the American moral project

HOWEVER, IT IS IMPOSSIBLE, on the basis of material and technological success alone, to form a credible picture of the American genius, or of the intellectual phenomena—the ideals of freedom, equality before the law, and justice—which have been passed down from generation to generation as a spiritual heritage with the strength of "destiny." America has always seen itself as a culture that recognizes individual accomplishment and merit, but in practice, indigenous Indians and Blacks brought to America by the slave trade did not enjoy equal rights with other Americans until the late twentieth century. Exclusion remained the norm, despite the many Black and Indian Americans who strove to help their people adapt to the dominant White culture, and the countless numbers who made the ultimate sacrifice and gave their lives in America's wars. The process of coming to terms with, and remedying, the individual and collective exclusion of particular social groups remains an existential issue in the United States. A historical overview of the treatment of Native Americans and Blacks is essential to

33

understand the tensions that characterize America today. As the previously cited George Friedman put it, "No discussion of the invention of the United States is permissible without addressing the glaring moral crimes of the nation."[1]

THE EXCLUSION OF BLACKS

The tensions and problems of conscience in Black–White relations in the modern United States are rooted in the historical fact of slavery. According to George Friedman, "The United States not only carried on the practice of slavery but defined Africans formally and legally as subhuman."[2] To illustrate the complexity of the problem, let us take as our example one of the most prominent personalities in American history: Thomas Jefferson was an erudite lawyer and Virginia planter who had an impressive career as a congressman, ambassador, secretary of state, vice president, and president of the United States. He argued tirelessly for the ideals of freedom, equality, and justice. He engraved the following slogan on his seal ring: "Rebellion to tyrants is obedience to God." In 1776, he drafted the famous lines in the Declaration of Independence: "life, liberty, and the pursuit of happiness."[3] In 1787, Jefferson voted for a constitution based on these principles: "We the people of the United States, in order to form a more perfect union, establish justice, ensure domestic tranquility, provide for the common defense, promote the general welfare, and secure the blessings of liberty to ourselves and our posterity, do ordain and establish this constitution for the United States of America."[4] In his inaugural address on March 4, 1801, he said that "a wise and frugal government, which shall restrain men from injuring one another, shall leave them otherwise free to regulate their own pursuits of industry and improvement, and shall not take from the mouth of labor the bread it has earned."[5]

However, until 1868, the Constitution considered slaves to be only three-fifths people: "Representatives and direct Taxes shall be apportioned among the several States which may be included within this Union, according to their respective Numbers, which shall be determined by adding to the whole Number of free Persons, including those bound to Service for a Term of Years, and excluding Indians not taxed, three fifths of all other Persons."[6] The term "other persons" referred to slaves, who were mentioned in the Constitution solely because there were fewer Whites in the South than in the Northern states, and without the inclusion of Blacks, the Southerners would not have been able to secure the same proportion of votes in the House of Representatives as the Northerners.

Slavery was common throughout the thirteen colonies, albeit in varying proportions. Jefferson, George Washington, and indeed almost all the Founding Fathers owned slaves, although they regularly wrote pamphlets condemning the institution of slavery. Jefferson blamed George III for the slave trade in his draft Declaration of Independence, saying that the king "has waged cruel war against human nature itself, violating its most sacred rights of life and liberty in the persons of a distant people who never offended him, captivating and carrying them into slavery in another hemisphere, or to incur miserable death in their transportation thither."[7] However, under pressure from the Southerners, this section, along with any mention of the term slavery, was expunged from the Declaration of Independence and the Constitution. Jefferson, by the way, unlike most of his contemporaries, considered the Indians to be "physically and intellectually" on an equal footing with the Whites, so long as they abandoned their culture and assimilated.[8] During Jefferson's presidency, a ban on the slave trade was passed in 1808, but it was to remain a dead letter. Moreover, as the law reduced external supply, or made it riskier, the price of slaves rose, making the "breeding and propagation" of slaves a new source of income for plantation owners. Jefferson never supported full emancipation, saying it would put Black people unable to take care of themselves in an even worse position. The Jefferson problem is succinctly captured in a famous remark by Dr. Samuel Johnson: "How is it that we hear the loudest yelps for liberty among the drivers of negroes?"[9]

As a politician, Jefferson certainly believed that his position on the question of slavery was reasonable. It was clear for him that the human good in the founding documents would not be available to Blacks, and that they would remain slaves. He probably believed that the practical achievement of important goals justified the betrayal of the letter and spirit of legislations and declarations, and indeed his own convictions. This is how the political rationalization of problems generally works: decisions that benefit a chosen community can have adverse consequences upon others.

However, Jefferson did not follow the convictions of a person condemning slavery in his personal life: he bought and sold slaves, and owned more than 600 slaves over the course of his lifetime. He did not free his slaves even after 1782, when this was permitted by the laws of Virginia, and about ten thousand slaves in the state were released shortly after the law came into force. After his death, in 1827, his heir had to sell 130 slaves to settle the debts of the estate. This problem cannot be rationalized: a rational and virtuous person can judge his or her own actions and their consequences, and is free to choose between good and evil. It was possible to own slaves while verbally condemning the practice, or to choose not to own slaves even when it was legally permitted.

Exceptional individuals, conscious of their own exceptionalism, may be tempted to believe that the rules of logic and morality do not apply in their own case. Although Jefferson, who sympathized with the French Jacobin ideologies, did not really believe in either God or religious teachings, he regularly cited the Bible. Surely, he often heard the verse that strengthened the colonial Protestants' sense of exceptionalism: "For whatsoever is born of God overcometh the world" (1 John 5:4). But Jefferson may have known that the Bible is a unity, and the words of John are valid along with the Gospel of Matthew: "For what is a man profited, if he shall gain the whole world, and lose his own soul? or what shall a man give in exchange for his soul?" (Matt. 16:26). There is hardly any sign in Jefferson's vast written legacy that he lamented or struggled with the dilemma of wealth and ease gained at the cost of depriving others. However, one particular diary entry indicates that he was aware of the sin: "Deep rooted prejudices entertained by the whites; ten thousand recollections, by the blacks, of the injuries they have sustained . . . will divide us into parties, and produce convulsions which will probably never end but in the extermination of the one or the other race. . . . I tremble for my country when I reflect that God is just, that his justice cannot sleep forever. . . . The Almighty has no attribute which can take side with us in such a contest."[10]

At the time of the founding of the United States, in 1790, there were nearly 700,000 Blacks—about 18

37

per cent of the population—living in slavery, while in 1860, the 4 million Black slaves and half a million free Blacks made up 14 per cent of the population. In the history of the North Atlantic slave trade, a total of 12 to 13 million slaves reached America alive. Slavery was concentrated: in 1860, only 5 per cent of Southern Whites owned a slave, and less than one per cent had more than a hundred slaves.[11]

Nothing compelled Americans to import slaves. Aside from their philosophical, moral, and religious concerns, they, of their own free will, maintained the institution of slavery for material gain. In Britain, on the other hand, as early as 1772, a certain judge, Lord Mansfield, ruled that slavery was untenable. In his judgment, refusing to return a slave who had fled his American master in England, he states: "The state of slavery is of such a nature that it is incapable of being introduced on any reasons, moral or political, but only by positive law, which preserves its force long after the reasons, occasions, and time itself from whence it was created, is erased from memory. It is so odious, that nothing can be suffered to support it, but positive law. Whatever inconveniences, therefore, may follow from the decision, I cannot say this case is allowed or approved by the law of England; and therefore the black must be discharged."[12]

Slavery was widespread throughout the world. However, unlike the American practice, a person who was enslaved as a prisoner of war, or through debt or purchase, was generally seen as belonging to the same species as his or her owner. In the Christian conception, a slave was considered equal to free persons in terms of God's creation. Therefore, in contemporary Spanish slavery, for example, the owner's rights over his slave were limited first by church law, and secondly by civil law, which recognized the slave as a "person" possessing dignity and certain rights. Thus, the enslaved or liberated slave did not carry inferior status as a stamp. Under American law, on the other hand, a slave was not classified as a person but as an object, and as such had no rights whatsoever. As a result, for example, the American Anglican Church long refused to baptize Blacks, and they were forbidden education and the right of assembly. Furthermore, as slavery and race overlapped, the stamps of inferiority remained on Blacks even after liberation, and the mulatto children of free White and unfree Black parents were also born into slave status because of their skin color. That is why Tocqueville was able to state that in America, "the immaterial and transitory fact of slavery combines in the most disastrous way with the material and permanent fact of racial difference. The memory of slavery dishonors the race, and race perpetuates the memory of slavery."[13]

In the debates which attended the founding of the United States, one political and two economic arguments were made in favor of slavery. The political argument was about whether it is possible to establish a federation while slavery remain. Nine of the thirteen colonies at the time had to vote "yes" for the Articles of Confederation to pass. The Founding Fathers feared that a failure to secure lasting federation could lead to war, both with outside European powers and between colonies, threatening unforeseeable human and material losses; therefore slavery was an acceptable price for peace and strength in unity. One of the economic arguments complementing this reasoning was that without the export of cotton, sugar cane, and tobacco, the US economy would collapse, but their production required slaves. The other economic reason was a well-known argument from ancient Greece: running public affairs is a time-consuming endeavor that only financially independent individuals can afford. This, in turn, presupposes wealth which is either inherited or based on the work of others, such as slaves. The Founding Fathers, based upon an opportunity cost calculation, decided that the political and economic benefits and advantages of federation outweighed the burdens and wrongs borne by the people forced into slavery. Tocqueville, an outside observer, considered these arguments and explanations, and came to the view widely held among Europeans that this was a self-perpetuating situation:

> From the moment that Europeans began to take slaves from another race of men, a race that many of them saw as inferior to the other human races and with which they could never contemplate assimilating without horror, they assumed that slavery was eternal. For between the extreme inequality created by slavery and the complete equality to which independence naturally leads, there is no durable intermediate state. Europeans were vaguely aware of this truth but never admitted it to themselves. Whenever the question of the Negro arose, they followed the dictates either of interest and pride or else of pity. With respect to the black man they violated all the rights of humanity and then schooled him in the value and inviolability of those rights.[14]

Nevertheless, many Whites condemned slavery. A 1790 resolution of the Society for the Promotion of Freedom and the Relief of Persons Holden in Bondage declared that "this trade and the consequent slavery" were "contrary to every principle of justice and humanity, of the law of nature and of the law of

God."[15] There were those who hoped that the spirit and letter of the Declaration of Independence would prevail sooner or later, and that the end of slavery was only a matter of time. In 1853, Theodore Parker, a White Unitarian pastor who actively advocated for equality, put it this way: "I do not pretend to understand the moral universe...the arc is a long one, my eye reaches but little ways.... But from what I see I am sure it bends towards justice."[16] From the early 1800s until the Civil War, specific plans were also formulated to address the issue of slavery. One such plan involved the repatriation of Blacks to Africa, but only a few thousand Black Americans reached Liberia, established in 1820, and the repatriation, partly due to the lack of interest among those to be sent, never materialized.

Some Black leaders still consider the United States a racist nation, while others, such as Frederick Douglass, who escaped in 1847, argued that the founding principles were essentially sound; the problem was with their implementation. Douglass added that political equality (equality before the law) does not necessarily mean cultural or ethnic parity. Hopes that slavery would be gradually abolished faded after a series of congressional, court and Supreme Court judgments broadened its legalization. In his famous "A House Divided" speech of June 16, 1858, Abraham Lincoln argued that slavery was not gradually fading away. On the contrary, it was gaining ground: "The new year of 1854 found slavery excluded from more than half the States by State constitutions, and from most of the national territory by congressional prohibition. Four days later commenced the struggle which ended in repealing that congressional prohibition. This opened all the national territory to slavery."[17]

THE GENIUS OF AMERICA

The complexity of the abolition of slavery is well illustrated by Stephen Douglas's argument in the seventh debate with Lincoln during the Senate elections on October 15, 1858:

> The signers of the Declaration of Independence had no reference to negroes at all when they declared all men to be created equal. They did not mean negro, nor the savage Indians, ... nor any other barbarous race.... They alluded to men of European birth and European descent—to white men.... It was established by white men for the benefit of white men and their posterity forever, and should be administered by white men, and none others. But it does not follow, by any means, that merely because the negro is not a citizen, and merely because he is not our equal, that, therefore, he should be a slave. On the contrary, it does follow that we ought to extend to the negro race, and to all other dependent races all the rights, all the privileges, and all the immunities which they can exercise consistently with the safety of society. Humanity requires that we should give them all these privileges; Christianity commands that we should extend those privileges to them. The question then arises what are those privileges, and what is the nature and extent of them. My answer is that that is a question which each State must answer for itself. We in Illinois have decided it for ourselves. We tried slavery, kept it up for twelve years, and finding that it was not profitable, we abolished it for that reason, and became a free State. We adopted in its stead the policy that a negro in this State shall not be a slave and shall not be a citizen. We have a right to adopt that policy.[18]

The issue was further nuanced by political considerations related to the functioning of democracy, as Lawrence Lowell, president of Harvard University, explained in a private letter in 1910: "We know that in order to win the election, Negroes in the southern states have been deprived of their rights.... As for the Chinese, we protected the homogeneity of the country from them by not giving them rights. I considered these measures bad when I was young, but now that we need homogeneity for democracy, I believe they were absolutely right."[19] Lowell publicly argued for gradual emancipation that did not threaten the nature of American society.

The changes began in the 1860s, following the end of the Civil War on April 9, 1865—a war which had claimed the lives of 700,000 people, amounting to some 2 per cent of a population of 31.5 million. Nearly a hundred years after the signing of the Declaration of Independence, the abolition of slavery was enshrined in the Constitution, citizens were granted citizenship, and their equality before the law was declared. However, the constitutional amendment only brought about a change in words. From 1896, the equality provisions of the constitutional amendments were formally applied by US courts under the doctrine of "separate but equal,"[20] meaning, in practice, segregation, until the 1950s. Segregation in American universities only ended in the late 1960s, though desegregation began as early as 1947 in the army.

The Southern Christian Leadership Conference was established in 1957 to "redeem the soul of America," that is, to achieve practical equality and end segregation. The culmination of this movement was Martin Luther King Jr.'s speech in 1963 in front of the Lincoln Memorial: "I have a dream that one day this nation will rise up and live out the true meaning of its creed: 'We hold these truths to be self-evident, that all men are created equal.'"[21] However, in 1967, nearly a hundred years after the rights of Black Americans were enshrined in the Constitution, in the face of violence against Blacks in the South and cold disdain from Whites in the North, King said in frustration: "It is necessary to refute the idea that the dominant ideology in our country, even today, is freedom and equality while racism is just an occasional departure from the norm on the part of a few bigoted extremists."[22] The constitutional amendments did not bring about fundamental change in the lives of Blacks, and the tensions between ideals and perceived reality can still spark open violence to this day. Despite enduring problems, it is undeniable that there has been a huge improvement in the upward social mobility of Black Americans, in all areas of life, from sport and the arts to business, science, and politics.

THE DISPOSSESSION AND ANNIHILATION OF THE INDIANS

Unlike Blacks, Indians had been living in America before the arrival of Europeans. The White Europeans, who thought in terms of private property, saw the whole continent and its resources as theirs by right. The Indians also considered these territories to be theirs, so Whites saw them as either prospective business partners or competitors to be overcome, and often as primitive and childish beings in need of guardianship. Proponents of partnership with the Indians initially won legal recognition of Indians' rights. The First Continental Congress, in its resolution of October 14, 1774, enshrined the general rights of Americans: "That the inhabitants of the English colonies in North-America, by the immutable laws of nature, the principles of the English constitution, and the several charters or compacts, have the following rights . . . they are entitled to life, liberty and property: and they have never ceded to any foreign power whatever, a right to dispose of either without their consent."[23] It was in this spirit that legislation governing Indians was passed in 1787: "The utmost good faith shall always be observed towards the Indians; their lands and property shall never be taken from them without their consent; and, in their property, rights, and liberty, they shall never be invaded or disturbed, unless in just and lawful wars authorized by Congress; but laws founded in justice and humanity, shall from time to time be made for preventing wrongs being done to them, and for preserving peace and friendship with them."[24]

However, the hungry Whites flocking to the West had a different idea of the rights of the Indians and the "immutable laws of nature." Congress and the government did not allocate adequate resources to enforce their own laws. A typical example is George Washington's presidential message to Congress on January 30, 1794:

> It appeared that the difficulties with the Creeks had been amicably and happily terminated. But it will be perceived, with regret, by the papers herewith transmitted, that the tranquility has unfortunately been of short duration, owing to the murder of several friendly Indians by some lawless white men. The condition of things in that quarter requires the serious and immediate consideration of Congress; and the adoption of such wise and vigorous laws, as will be competent to the preservation of the national character, and of the peace, made under the authority of the United States, with the several Indian tribes. Experience demonstrates that the existing legal provisions are entirely inadequate to those great objects.[25]

The laws were made with the best of intentions, but there was no federal will or power to enforce them. White people who supported living alongside the Indians were simply swept out of the way.

The total number of North American Indians before 1492 is estimated at 3.8–4.4 million.[26] By comparison, the population of the United States (excluding Indians) was ten million in 1820. Census data on Indians living in the United States is only available from 1900, when 237,000 people declared themselves to be Indians, compared to three million Indians and Indigenous Alaskans in 2010, and a further 2.3 million people who claimed some Native American descent.[27] After 1492, the Indian population declined drastically due to plagues and other illnesses, as well as White violence.

There were also some examples of successful coexistence. In Pennsylvania, under the terms of equitable treaties offered by William Penn in 1628, the Lenape Indians and Quakers lived side by side in Christian partnership. This peaceable existence proved viable for more than a hundred years, but after Penn's death, his descendants fraudulently annulled and falsified treaties, and dispossessed the Indians. However, there were also countless examples not only of coexistence, but even of cohabitation, especially between frontier White men and Indian women. Later, during the War of Independence, Americans loyal to the British Crown found refuge and wives with the Indians, and in the nineteenth century, Northern Europeans, who inhabited the northern regions of the Midwest, also mingled with the Indians:

> The French too often grew passionately fond of the state of wild freedom they found them in. They became the most dangerous of the inhabitants of the desert and won the friendship of the Indian

46

by exaggerating his vices and his virtues. M. de Senonville, the governor of Canada, wrote thus to Louis XIV in 1685: "It has long been believed that in order to civilize the savages we ought to draw them nearer to us. But there is every reason to suppose we have been mistaken. Those which have been brought into contact with us have not become French, and the French who have lived among them are changed into savages, affecting to dress and live like them."[28]

Despite examples of coexistence, the Indians gradually had to face the fact that it was impossible for Whites to live peacefully alongside them, or to keep their promises and covenants. Tribes fought desperate defensive wars to preserve their territories.[29] However, they were unable to maintain lasting alliances with one another. Hence from the seventeenth to the nineteenth centuries they were ruthlessly exploited by the British, Americans, and French, who turned the tribes against each other in brutal, internecine wars on the top of the fights the Indians exacted against each other anyway. The Whites sought to retaliate for the Indians' defensive efforts, and were not squeamish about the means of doing so. They launched systematic killing campaigns, in which a blood price was paid first for each decapitated Indian head, and later for each scalp.[30] On April 14, 1756, Governor Robert Morris, declaring war on the Delaware Indians in the pages of the Pennsylvania Gazette, offered "$150 for each male prisoner above the age of twelve years, or $130 for a corresponding scalp: $130 for a male prisoner under the age of twelve, or a female prisoner; and $50 for the scalp of an Indian woman."[31] In 1755, the governor of Massachusetts, William Shirley, offered "for every male prisoner above twelve years of age, £40. For every scalp of any male above twelve years of age, that shall be brought as evidence of his death, £38. For every female prisoner, and each male prisoner, under twelve years of age, £20. For every scalp of such female or male, under twelve years of age, £19."[32] £40 would be equivalent to £7,400 in 2011 purchasing value.[33] This blood money proved a strong incentive, as is apparent from the Remonstrance of the Pennsylvania Frontiersmen of February 13, 1764, written by Matthew Smith and James Gibson: "In the late Indian war this province, with others of his Majesty's colonies, gave rewards for Indian scalps, to encourage the seeking them in their own country as the most likely means of destroying or reducing them to reason, but no such encouragement has been given in this war, which has damped the spirits of many brave men who are willing, to venture their lives in parties against the enemy. We, therefore, pray that public rewards may be proposed for Indian scalps, which may be adequate to the dangers attending enterprises of this nature."[34] In addition to the blood price paid for scalps, a form of biological warfare was also employed against the Indians. British Commander Jeffrey Amherst also authorized the use of all means, including blankets infected with smallpox, to combat them: "You will do well to infect the Indians by means of blankets, as well as try every other method that can serve to extirpate this execrable race."[35]

The Indians achieved temporary success until the 1830s, but they could only postpone the inevitable westward advance of the settlers. The French had sold the Louisiana territory to the Americans in 1803, and with the Anglo-American peace treaty in Ghent in 1814, it became apparent that the British had finally acknowledged the independence of the United States.

The fate of the Indians, who relied on alliances with the French or British, had thus been sealed.

The Americans viewed the seizure of Native American territories as lawful. In the seventeenth century, the doctrine of no-man's land (*terra nullius* or *vacuum domicilium*), incorrectly associated with the work of John Locke,[36] became popular, according to which man is responsible for exploiting natural resources, and no man has a right to restrict another in this unless it harms his own livelihood. This view was in line with the Puritans' deep antipathy towards sloth and waste. In the words of Francis Higginson and Robert Cushman of New England: "The Indians are not able to make use of the one fourth part of the land, neither have they any settled places, as towns to dwell in, nor any ground as they challenge for their own possession, but change their habitation from place to place .... As the ancient patriarchs therefore removed from straiter places into more roomy, where the land lay idle, and none used it, though there dwelt inhabitants by them ... so it is lawful now to take a land which none useth, and make use of it."[37]

In his first congressional address in 1817, President James Monroe argued in a similar vein: "The earth was given to mankind to support the greatest number of which it is capable, and no tribe or people have a right to withhold from the wants of others more than is necessary for their own support and comfort."[38] Monroe was concerned about violence against Indians, and in December of the same year he authorized federal funds to protect them and support their transition to agriculture, as well as their introduction to "the arts of civilized life." However, rates of violence did not decrease. Finally, in 1825, Monroe proposed relocating them to areas west of Mississippi:

For the removal of the tribes within the limits of the State of Georgia the motive has been peculiarly strong, arising from the compact with that State whereby the United States are bound to extinguish the Indian title to the lands within it whenever it may be done peaceably and on reasonable conditions.... The removal of the tribes from the territory which they now inhabit...would not only shield them from impending ruin, but promote their welfare and happiness. Experience has clearly demonstrated that in their present state it is impossible to incorporate them in such masses, in any form whatever, into our system. It has also demonstrated with equal certainty that without a timely anticipation of and provision against the dangers to which they are exposed, under causes which it will be difficult, if not impossible to control, their degradation and extermination will be inevitable.[39]

Just nineteen days after President Andrew Jackson took office, on March 23, 1829, he sent the following letter to the leaders of the Creek Indians: "Beyond the great river Mississippi, where a part of your nation has gone, your father has provided a country large enough for all of you, and he advises you to remove to it. There your white brothers will not trouble you; they will have no claim to the land, and you can live upon it, you and all your children, as long as the grass grows, or the water runs, in peace and plenty. It will be yours forever."[40] When the resettlement law was introduced in December 1830, Jackson delivered the following address:

We now propose to acquire the countries occupied by the red men of the South and West by a fair exchange, and, at the expense of the United States, to send them to land where their existence may be prolonged and perhaps made perpetual. Doubtless it

will be painful to leave the graves of their fathers;
but what do they more than our ancestors did or
than our children are now doing? To better their
condition in an unknown land our forefathers left all
that was dear in earthly objects.... Does Humanity
weep at these painful separations from everything,
animate and inanimate, with which the young heart
has become entwined? Far from it. It is rather a
source of joy that our country affords scope where
our young population may range unconstrained in
body or in mind, developing the power and facilities
of man in their highest perfection.... Can it be
cruel in this Government when, by events which it
cannot control, the Indian is made discontented in
his ancient home to purchase his lands, to give him
a new and extensive territory, to pay the expense
of his removal, and support him a year in his new
abode? How many thousands of our own people
would gladly embrace the opportunity of removing
to the West on such conditions! If the offers made
to the Indians were extended to them, they would
be hailed with gratitude and joy. And is it supposed
that the wandering savage has a stronger attachment
to his home than the settled, civilized Christian?[41]

The treaties that had governed relations between
the federal government and the sovereign tribes from
the 1780s to 1832 were unilaterally abolished. On June
30, 1834, the "Indian Territory" was established in
what is now Oklahoma. Tens of thousands of Indians
were driven along the thousand-mile-long "Trail of
Tears" through Mississippi to Oklahoma. Those driven
along this route included the civilized Creek, Choctaw,
Chickasaw, and Seminole tribes, who had believed that
if they assimilated, they would be left alone in their
land. The biggest losers were the Cherokee, who had
long since converted to farming and lived according to

white customs, with the white education system and a daily newspaper, swore allegiance to the Constitution, and fought under the American flag. Tocqueville assessed the situation in 1831 as follows:

> The conduct of the Americans of the United States toward the Indians exhibits the purest love of formalities and legalities. Provided that the Indians remain in the savage state, the Americans do not interfere in their affairs and treat them as independent peoples. They will not occupy Indian land until it has been duly acquired by contract. And if by chance an Indian nation can no longer live within its territory, the Americans offer a fraternal hand and lead the natives off to die somewhere other than in the land of their fathers. The Spaniards, despite acts of unparalleled monstrousness that left them indelibly covered with shame, were unable to exterminate the Indian race or even prevent the Indians from sharing their rights. The Americans of the United States achieved both results with marvelous ease, quietly, legally, philanthropically, without bloodshed, without violating a single one of the great principles of morality in the eyes of the world. To destroy human beings with greater respect for the laws of humanity would be impossible.[42]

Famine then struck Oklahoma, and tribal lands also became a target. In 1877, Congress passed the Desert Land Act, which paved the way for the parceling out of publicly owned land in the West. The Indians were no longer members of a collective tribe, but individual owners, and this change paved the way for the Whites to acquire land inside reservations.

The remnants of the free Indians, the Sioux, Crow, Blackfoot, Cheyenne, and Arapaho in the north, and the Apache in the southwest, were hunted down by both settlers and the regular army of the United States.

The case of Colonel John Chivington shows the depth of the hatred felt for the Indians. At Sand Creek on November 29, 1864, while the Civil War was still raging, Chivington and his seven hundred volunteer soldiers slaughtered 230 Cheyenne and Arapaho Indians, mostly women and children, who had already surrendered their weapons. The next day the corpses were cruelly mutilated: "Damn any man who sympathizes with Indians!...I have come to kill Indians, and believe it is right and honorable to use any means under God's heaven to kill Indians.... Kill and scalp all, big and little; nits make lice!"[43] A military investigation revealed that one in seven volunteers refused the massacre order. Captain Silas Soule, who testified in the investigation against Chivington, was shot three months later in Denver. His killers' identities were known, but they were never brought to justice.[44]

The Indians struggled on a while longer, but at last gave up the fight after their resources were exhausted. On October 5, 1877, Chief Joseph of the Nez Percé tribe, also known as "The Red Napoleon," surrendered to a force thirty times larger than his own, led by General Oliver Howard. Two years later, in 1879, at the invitation of the president, he traveled to Washington. This is how he summarized his experience:

> I am glad I came. I have shaken hands with a good many friends, but there are some things I want to know which no one seems able to explain. I cannot understand how the Government sends a man out to fight us, as it did General Miles, and then breaks his word. I have seen the Great Father Chief [President Hayes]; the Next Great Chief [Secretary of the Interior]; the Commissioner Chief [Commissioner of Indian Affairs]; the Law Chief [General Butler]; and many other law chiefs

[Congressmen] and they all say they are my friends, and that I shall have justice, but while all their mouths talk right I do not understand why nothing is done for my people. I have heard talk and talk but nothing is done. Good words do not last long unless they amount to something. Words do not pay for my dead people. They do not pay for my country now overrun by white men. They do not protect my father's grave. They do not pay for my horses and cattle. Good words do not give me back my children. I am tired of talk that comes to nothing. If the white man wants to live in peace with the Indian he can live in peace. There need be no trouble. Treat all men alike. Give them the same laws. Give them all an even chance to live and grow. All men were made by the same Great Spirit Chief. They are all brothers. The earth is the mother of all people, and all people should have equal rights upon it. I have asked some of the Great White Chiefs where they get their authority to say to the Indian that he shall stay in one place, while he sees white men going where they please. They cannot tell me. When I think of our condition, my heart is heavy. I see men of my own race treated as outlaws and driven from country to country, or shot down like animals. I know that my race must change. We cannot hold our own with the white men as we are. We only ask an even chance to live as other men live. We ask to be recognized as men. Let me be a free man, free to travel, free to stop, free to work, free to trade where I choose, free to choose my own teachers, free to follow the religion of my fathers, free to talk, think and act for myself—and I will obey every law or submit to the penalty. I hope no more groans of wounded men and women will ever go to the ear of the Great Spirit Chief above, and that all people may be one people.[45]

His words were recorded, but "the beautiful words departed, and deeds did not follow them."

The Indians' problem stemmed from the fact that they did not even understand the Whites' way of thinking, or their view of space and time. In spatial terms, they did not understand the notion of private property beyond personal use, since they felt they had infinite space, and were not tormented by envy, a sense of lack, or acquisitive desires in the way that those from crowded Europe or the east coast of America were. Indian tribes also engaged in constant warfare, out of interest or fear, honor or pride. Similar motives sparked European wars, of course, but there the ultimate goal was to gain territory and resources with it. The Indians regarded the earth as the same as air or water—something everyone could use as need required. Furthermore, the Indians were not individualists, but saw the life of the individual in time as fitting into an endless cycle of generations. They believed that the spirits of the dead live inseparably with the living on their specific common land and territory. That was why they insisted on remaining so close to the graves of their ancestors. This was diametrically opposed to the ideas of the Whites, who strove ever to expand and improve their material wealth through progress. How could a White man who had left his homeland multiple times and abandoned the ways of his ancestors have understood the attachment of some savages to the graves of their forebears?

The Indians did not acquire all the civil rights held by other Americans until the last third of the twentieth century. Although Indian veterans were granted citizenship from 1919, and this was extended to all Indians in 1924, the right to vote was granted only in 1965. Indians won the right to freedom of expression, recourse to the courts, and protection against unjustified search and detention only in 1968. George Friedman summarizes what happened: "The United States violated almost all of those treaties. This was an integral part of the crime. Americans were not responsible for the complex politics and warfare waged by Indian nations against other Indian nations. Nor were Americans responsible for the disease they brought. But they were guilty of confronting Indian nations and waging war and then systematically betraying them in every way possible in making peace. In so doing, the United States turned a bearable defeat into total dispossession of an Indian population."[46]

❧

CHAPTER FIVE

The problem of reconciling American ideals and practice

FROM THE PERSPECTIVE OF THE American genius, the world looks like this: America is an unparalleled country rich in natural resources, where individuals driven by a desire for improvement, adventure, power and profit compete for resources. Starting with a clean slate, Americans, building on the accumulated experience of humanity, have established a political order based on freedom, equality before the law, and justice founded upon practical reason. The key to prosperity is that everybody acts following well-conceived interests, and all are the authors of their own fortune. This rational order affords those with ability the best opportunity there has ever been to live a life of human dignity and prosperity. America offers opportunities to anyone, regardless of ethnic and religious identity, so long as they accept the demands of utilitarian competition and do not violate the freedom of others. Proof of the system's effectiveness is the country's impressive material and technological performance by global standards. Americans rightly regard their ideals as universal, either as a "divine commandment," or as "Manifest Destiny," and consider the American experiment as exceptional in the history of mankind.

However, the practical application of American ideals is often limited. In some cases, there may be insufficient resources to extend those ideals, while some may be excluded from the benefits they promise. Nor is it rare for certain peoples or nations to reject the ideals from the outset. The phenomenon whereby people cling to ideals even when their actual circumstances or actions directly contradict them is known in psychology as cognitive dissonance, that is, a person who does not act in accordance with his or her believed and stated ideals, but instead seeks to rationalize the contradiction in order to preserve his or her inner integrity, identity, and ability to act. In his 1944 work *An American Dilemma: The Negro Problem and Modern Democracy*, Gunnar Myrdal argues that Whites are not cynical about their beliefs, but keep their ideals and their actual behavior in two separate mental compartments:

> As people's valuations are conflicting, behavior normally becomes a moral compromise. There are no homogeneous "attitudes" behind human behavior but a mesh of struggling inclinations, interests, and ideals, some held conscious and some suppressed for long intervals but all active in bending behavior in their direction.... We shall find that even a poor and uneducated white person in some isolated and backward rural region in the Deep South, who is violently prejudiced against the Negro and intent upon depriving him of civic rights and human independence, has also a whole compartment in his valuation sphere housing the entire American Creed of liberty, equality, justice, and fair opportunity for everybody. He is actually also a good Christian and honestly devoted to the ideals of human brotherhood and the Golden Rule.[1]

The contradiction between ideals and political practice can perhaps best be understood by studying the
thoughts of Abraham Lincoln. Lincoln had a Christian
upbringing, but by the time he was a young adult he
had become less interested in religion. Later, following
several family tragedies,[2] his wife and closest associates
reported that he became more and more preoccupied
with the will of God, reading the Bible daily, praying a
great deal, and attending worship frequently at the Pres-
byterian Church on New York Avenue, a ten-minute
walk from the White House. From his speeches, cor-
respondence, and notes, it is clear that his mindset was
characterized by a harmonious balance of rationality and
belief in Providence. He believed in American ideals,
was convinced that America could not be realistically
threatened by any external power, and felt that danger
could only arise from within. Referring to slavery in
1838, he put it this way: "At what point then is the
approach of danger to be expected? I answer, if it ever
reach us, it must spring up amongst us. It cannot come
from abroad. If destruction be our lot, we must ourselves be its author and finisher. As a nation of freemen,
we must live through all time, or die by suicide."[3] Lincoln did not merely speak of "danger" in the abstract,
but called it out specifically. In 1855, for example, he
said the following: "As a nation we began by declaring
that, 'All men are created equal.' ... When the Know
Nothings get control, it will read, 'All men are created
equal, except Negroes and foreigners and Catholics.'
When it comes to this, I shall prefer immigrating to
some country where they make no pretense of loving
liberty—to Russia, for instance, where despotism can
be taken pure and without the base alloy of hypocrisy."[4]

The Civil War was already raging when, in his
presidential speech to Congress in 1862, he stated his

continued belief that the United States was "the last best hope of earth,"[5] and that it was up to the common sense of Americans to make it work. He repeatedly pointed out that he believed there was such a thing as divine truth, which one must seek to recognize and follow, but which does not absolve one of responsibility for one's actions, because man cannot confer that upon God. He wrote and talked extensively about the dangers of American complacency: "We have been the recipients of the choicest bounties of Heaven; we have been preserved these many years in peace and prosperity; we have grown in numbers, wealth, and power.... But we have forgotten God. Intoxicated with unbroken success, we have become too self-sufficient to feel the necessity of redeeming and preserving grace, too proud to pray to the God that made us."[6] In 1865, 36 days before the end of the Civil War, he was re-elected as president. In his inaugural speech, he emphasized once again that the invocation of divine truth could not absolve him from final judgement:

> Neither party expected for the war the magnitude or the duration which it has already attained.... Both read the same Bible and pray to the same God and each invokes His aid against the other.... The prayers of both could not be answered—that of neither has been answered fully. The Almighty has His own purposes: "Woe unto the world because of offences! for it must needs be that offences come; but woe to that man by whom the offence cometh!" Fondly do we hope—fervently do we pray—that this mighty scourge of war may speedily pass away. We can pray for the scandals to pass. Yet, if God wills that it continue... as was said three thousand years ago so still it must be said: "the judgments of the Lord are true and righteous altogether."[7]

Lincoln pointed to the cognitive dissonance between ideals and practice—which he called "scandal"—in a number of contexts. Despite his arguments for sobriety and humility before God, Americans have always been characterized by the same sense of mission once possessed by Athens, Rome, and London, a desire for profit, power and property, rather than Jerusalem's fear of God. It is as if we come across a modern version of the arguments known as the "Melian dialogue," recorded by the ancient Greek historian Thucydides. The Athenians issued the following ultimatum to the leaders of the polis of Melos:

> As for the Gods, we expect to have quite as much of their favour as you: for we are not doing or claiming anything which goes beyond common opinion about divine or men's desires about human things. For the Gods we believe, and of men we know, that by a law of their nature wherever they can rule they will. This law is not made by us, and we are not the first who have acted upon it; we did but inherit it, and shall bequeath it to all time, and we know that you and all mannkind, if you were as strong as we are, would do as we do. So much for the Gods; we have told you why we expect to stand as high in their good opinion as you.... But you and we should say what we really think, and aim only at what is possible, for we both alike know that into the discussion of human affairs the question of justice only enters where the pressure of necessity is equal, and that the powerful exact what they can, and the weak grant what they must.... And we will now endeavour to show that we have come in the interests of our empire, and that in what we are about to say we are only seeking the preservation of your city. For we want to make you ours with the least trouble

to ourselves, and it is for the interests of us both that you should not be destroyed.[8]

The Melians did not give up their city, so the Athenians occupied it after months of siege, killed the men, and sold the women and children into slavery.

The realist Tocqueville also concluded that the clash between ideals and practice was hardly a uniquely American phenomenon, but a part of the world's eternal logic:

> If all nations were small and none were large, humanity would surely be freer and happier. But one cannot prevent the existence of great nations. This introduces into the world a new element of national prosperity, namely, force. What does it matter if a nation presents an image of prosperity and freedom if it is constantly vulnerable to pillage and conquest? What good does it do a nation to excel in manufacturing and commerce if another country rules the seas and imposes its laws on markets everywhere? Small nations are often miserable not because they are small but because they are weak; large ones prosper not because they are large but because they are strong. For all nations, therefore, force is often a precondition of prosperity and even of existence. Barring unusual circumstances, therefore, small nations always end up annexed to great ones, either coerced by violence or of their own volition. I know of no condition more deplorable than that of a nation that cannot defend itself or supply its own needs. The federal system was created in order to combine the various advantages of largeness with those of smallness.[9]

In the light of the arguments of Thucydides, Tocqueville, and Lincoln, in the case of American cognitive dissonance, we must distinguish between Tocqueville's "necessary" use of force in order to grow, the moral judgment of the methods used, and the final judgement (before God) of Lincoln. Take, for example, the Indians, who since time immemorial had been content with the abundant resources of nature, and did not develop the technical and organizational skills that would have increased their numbers and strength, and which, for instance, might have made it possible to resist the Europeans. In Indian cultures, material equality was better realized, and they led a more unified way of life than those in White societies, but the price they paid was that individual talent and abilities could only be developed and employed in ways strictly defined by the community. Those who stepped out of line risked exclusion, and so any innovation ran into cultural barriers. Thus, looking back at the history of relations between the Indians and Whites, it was both inevitable and "necessary" in Tocqueville's sense that Whites would displace the Indians over time. However, this should in no way temper our moral condemnation of the cruel deeds committed by some Whites and some Indians.

Through numerical and technical superiority, and sheer capability, the Americans swept aside not only the Indians, but also European powers seeking their fortune in the New World. Take, for example, the case of the Spaniards, who once ruled far beyond the Rio Grande and who, confident of their superiority, themselves sought to civilize or destroy the canyon-dwelling Pueblo Indians. Over time, like the French among the Indians, the Spaniards' way of life became ever more distant from the standards of Madrid or even Mexico City, and came ever more closely to resemble the lives of the Mexican and Southwest Indians struggling simply to survive. Mexico became

independent of Spain in 1821, but the formerly Spanish Mexicans were unable to maintain or recreate the
political, economic, cultural, and military organization
of the motherland. Hardworking and sharp-elbowed
American craftsmen, entrepreneurs, and merchants
poured into the valley of the Rio Grande, building
roads, towns, farms, and factories. Within a few
decades they were the dominant power in the country-
side. Instead of competing with them, the New-World
Spaniards surrendered to feelings of insult, envy, and
self-pity, which over time developed into an inferiority complex toward the Yankees. Increasing numbers
of conflicts led to the Texas Revolution of 1835–36,
and culminated in the Mexican-American War of
1846–48, which resulted in Mexico losing about half
of its territory, while the victorious Americans took
over parts of present-day California, Nevada, Utah,
Colorado, New Mexico, Wyoming, and parts of Arizo-
na.[10] Here too, in hindsight, the Yankee victory over
the Mexicans seems inevitable, on account of their
technical superiority and capability. However, this
fact does not invalidate the devastating moral verdict
on the actions of both parties in the notoriously cruel
Mexican-American War.

On one side of the balance sheet, then, is the
"necessity" for individuals, endowed with reason and
free will, to unleash their potential for the benefit of
themselves and their communities. The fundamental
interest of the community lies in fostering individual
development, as the availability of more goods and
resources can help the community grow and reduce
violence and misery. Successful people who manage
their talents well feel proven, strong and capable, and
thus their communities are strengthened. As a result,
they consider it justified to recommend or force their

neighbors to adopt the methods and way of life that have led to their success. The notion of "Manifest Destiny" merely provides a moral framework for the preexisting physical and mental capabilities of Americans, which could only have been halted by greater strength or a more attractive alternative.[11] On the other side of the balance sheet are the suffering, loss, grief, and pain of those who, from lack of resources or ambition, are unable or unwilling to engage in the opportunities of the age and who, in our case, are subsumed by history and the American flag.

Thus, Tocqueville's argument that strength is a "necessary" precondition for prosperity and freedom seems logical and convincing, while it also appears clear that the crimes committed in the use of force are morally reprehensible, and their prevention or punishment can likewise only be achieved through strength. Historical experience has shown that no lasting institutional solution has been developed to prevent immoral acts, and that whether well-intentioned or malicious actors are in power, no such solution is realistically expected in the foreseeable future. A dynamic society cannot exist without the hunger for profit, property, power and adventure, employing the mental and physical abilities that are humanity's birthright. It is only possible to curb the hubris, arrogance, insatiability, and exaggerations that inevitably emerge as a result of these by limiting individuals' power of action, which, however, leads to a decline in the dynamism of a given community over time, and can lead to tyranny. At the same time, the recognition that the performance of individual social entities can be judged in the light of other existing alternatives cannot justify immorality and cruelty committed for the purposes—or on the pretext—of success. And finally there is still the ultimate judgement (by God) above necessity and moral law. Or in the words Lincoln cited, "Woe unto the world because of offences! for it must needs be that offences come; but woe to that man by whom the offence cometh!" (Matt. 18:7).[12] To this we may add Jefferson's self-reflection: "I tremble for my country when I reflect that God is just: that his justice cannot sleep for ever."[13]

CHAPTER SIX

❦

The American Genius Today

VISIONS OF AMERICA'S PRESENT AND FUTURE IN THE WORLD

ESPITE FREQUENT CHANGES of power, until the 2000s it appeared that both the Republican and Democratic parties, and the opinion-forming elite, shared fundamentally similar ideals of freedom, equality before the law, and justice. In this regard, until recently the United States, regardless of the political affiliation of the current president or the makeup of the Senate and the House of Representatives, faced the world with a broadly consistent stance. This predictable political consensus is now falling apart, with vastly different views on the meaning of ideals, the future of the United States, and the methods to be employed in reaching that future, domestically and abroad. The longstanding differences in attitude between the two sides have now escalated into a tribal cultural struggle of an existential nature, spilling over into everyday life beyond the realm of politics, and undermining the predictability of the United States internationally.

On one side of the dividing line we find the Democrats, who fit into the Puritan, Jacobin, Marxist, left-liberal tradition, while on the other we find the Republicans and their adherents, rooted in the classical (Ancient Greek and Roman) and biblical (Judeo-Christian) traditions of classical liberalism and Republican conservatism. One might say that it is an oversimplifying depiction of traditions that themselves are in debate or even conflict with each other about many topics in relation to the human person and society. Paul Johnson in his book *Intellectuals* explains why such a grouping is still valid and can inform further analysis.

> Over the past two hundred years the influence of intellectuals has grown steadily.... Seen against the long perspective of history it is in many ways a new phenomenon. It is true that in their earlier incarnations as priests, scribes and soothsayers, intellectuals have laid claim to guide society from the very beginning. But as guardians of hieratic cultures, whether primitive or sophisticated, their moral and ideological innovations were limited by the canons of external authority and by the inheritance of tradition. They were not, and could not be, free spirits, adventurers of the mind. With the decline of clerical power in the eighteenth century, a new kind of mentor emerged to fill the vacuum and capture the ear of society. The secular intellectual might be deist, sceptic or atheist. But he was just as ready as any pontiff or presbyter to tell mankind how to conduct its affairs. He proclaimed, from the start, a special devotion to the interests of humanity and an evangelical duty to advance them by his teaching. He brought to this self-appointed task a far more radical approach than his clerical predecessors.... The collective wisdom of the past, the legacy of tradition, the prescriptive codes of ancestral experience existed to be selectively followed or wholly rejected entirely as his own good sense might decide. For the first time in human history, and with growing confidence and audacity,

men arose to assert that they could diagnose the ills of society and cure them with their own unaided intellects: more, that they could devise formulae whereby not merely the structure of society but the fundamental habits of human beings could be transformed for the better.[1]

Hence, the difference between the two approaches is reflected in their conceptions of 'person' on the one hand, and of society on the other. According to the Puritan, Jacobin, Marxist, left-liberal creed, man can be perfected, and it is the task of the state to develop individuals in the direction of perfection. Conservatives, on the other hand, see human nature as inherently flawed and imperfect, so they place their trust in the slow and imperfect change of traditions, and reject the idea that the government knows what is good for people better than they themselves do. In addition to these matters of content, the gap between the camps is also growing in terms of methods. In place of a cumbersome, consensus-building culture, the practice of violent conflict is gaining ground in American public life.

THE WORLDVIEW OF THE PURITAN, JACOBIN, MARXIST, LEFT-LIBERAL TRADITION

The essence of the Puritan, Jacobin, Marxist, left-liberal tradition can be summarized as follows: man can be perfected, and the ideals to be achieved can be interpreted and realized through the collective. The unenlightened mass is unable to comprehend its own interests, so the role of a vanguard chosen by reason of their superior intellect and high morality is to determine what is good for the people. It is the task of the bureaucrats of the administrative state to implement the "social contract" in an impartial manner. This will put an end to political struggles, bring everlasting peace, and end history. For the individual, happiness can be ensured through devoted, obedient service to the common good, as dictated by the vanguard. The vanguard determines who "truly" understands the meaning of history, and the extent to which commons can share in material and political wealth. According to the Puritan, Jacobin, Marxist, and modern left-liberal, the unfortunate, backward, down-to-earth man who refuses to accept the promise of a bright future or simply "has a different vision of the future," is actually a sinner, deplorable, doomed to the dustbin of history, hence to be deprived of his property and expelled from society. According to this view, the history of America is a history of injustice, characterized by freedom for the few and inequality for the many.

Proponents of the Marxist/left-liberal position want to redefine the access of certain social groups to the blessings of freedom, equality, and justice, in order to eliminate injustices and achieve true freedom. They also reject both the ancient tradition of natural law and the Kantian foundation of the Enlightenment, according to which there are absolute ethical norms that apply to all human beings. Exclusion, rather than engagement, is seen as the means of solving social problems. They see the key to freedom in the radical transformation of social institutions and hierarchies. For instance, in the 1960s, Michel Foucault espoused the idea that authority is a disguise for freedom-restricting power, and that therefore, in the interests of true freedom, authority must be shorn of its mask and destroyed, thereby destroying repressive power.

Theoretical and methodological radicalization began to gain ground in America in the 1920s and 1930s, while until then the opportunity for growth based

on individual effort had provided a sufficient incentive and life goal for most people. Belief in individual
effort was stronger than the urge to blame others or
adverse circumstances for one's failures, and so even
those who could not keep up with the average level
of prosperity seldom turned against the social order.
After the Great Depression of 1929–33, countless charity programs were launched to help those left behind,
and to alleviate racial, economic, and political tensions.
Governments sought to integrate those living in impoverished regions or deprived metropolitan areas through
welfare programs, while churches and congregations
did the same through local community building. At
the same time, there was a proliferation of small but
vocal groups arguing that the path to effective integration and growth lay through conflict and unrest.
In the United States, the Marxists, imported from
Europe, and who came to dominate academia, were
at the forefront of efforts to promote radicalization
from the 1960s on. Herbert Marcuse played a prominent role in developing the theoretical background of
the violent approach, and Saul Alinsky, a "community organizer and radical activist," was a key figure
in the development of the practical methodology. To
understand the left-liberal mindset, we need to become
familiar with their ideas.

In his first book, *Reveille for Radicals*, published
in 1946, Alinsky wrote: "They [the radicals] are a
people creating a new bridge of mankind in between
the past of narrow nationalistic chauvinism and the
horizon of a new mankind—a people of the world.
Their face is the face of the future."[2] He summarized the job description of an agitator: "rub raw the
resentments of the people of the community; fan the
latent hostilities of many of the people to the point

of overt expression. He must search out controversy and issues, rather than avoid them.... An organizer must stir up dissatisfaction and discontent; provide a channel into which people can angrily pour their frustrations. He must create a mechanism that can drain off the underlying guilt for having accepted the previous situation for so long a time. Out of this mechanism, a new community organization arises."3 He believed that radicalized people would be able to make an impact if they organized themselves and took positions of power: "Organizations must be polarized first, even though people see conflict as a negative thing and think consensus is better."4 In order to provoke conflict, it is essential to designate the enemy, person or organization to whom the grievances are attributable and who must be defeated.

By the end of the 1960s, Alinsky was forced to face the lack of success in his efforts to provoke revolts and radicalize local communities. Violence made it very difficult to return to the negotiating table later, although at times he did succeed in having financial resources directed to some communities. However, his uncompromising approach resulted in only a few lasting improvements, and in most cases power was regained by the old structures, as well as gangs, usu- rers, and other exploiters. Alinsky consistently rejected compromise as a solution, maintaining that a commu- nity could only negotiate efficiently from a position of demonstrable power.5 In the last years of his life, he came to the conclusion that the vehicle of real change might be the middle class rather than the destitute poor, since through the former there was a greater opportu- nity to influence national politics. However, in order to steer the middle class in the right direction, it was first necessary to inculcate in them the idea of radical freedom. He also explained in a 1967 speech that "a free man is one who breaks the spatial and temporal constraints of security and status, and embarks on a life adventure characterized by passion, drama, risk, danger, creative pleasures, and the ability to change with the changes."[6] Hillary Rodham (later Clinton), who wrote her university dissertation "Analysis of the Alinsky Method" in 1969, represents Alinsky's work as that of a hero of democracy:

> In spite of his being featured in the Sunday New York Times and living a comfortable, expenses-paid life, he considers himself a revolutionary. In a very important way he is. If the ideals Alinsky espouses were actualized, the result would be social revolution. Ironically, this is not a disjunctive projection if considered in the tradition of Western democratic theory.... Alinsky is regarded by many as the proponent of a dangerous socio/political philosophy. As such, he has been feared—just as Eugene Debs or Walt Whitman or Martin Luther King has been feared, because each embraced the most radical of political faiths—democracy.[7]

Left-liberals believe that democracy and freedom are radical notions, and that radical means and methods must be employed to realize them. A theoretical program for this was published by Herbert Marcuse in his work *Repressive Tolerance* in 1965.[8]

According to Marcuse, liberal representative democracy is outdated and harmful, because in this system people are lulled into torpor by commercial propaganda. Propaganda fuels the illusion of material advancement, so that people cannot use their intellectual abilities. It also goes against the people's true interests, and hence they passively tolerate indoctrination and the violations of rights in the name of the *status quo*.

"What is proclaimed and practiced as tolerance today [1965], is . . . serving the cause of oppression . . . . It is the task and duty of the intellectual . . . to break the concreteness of oppression . . . on the road to affluence or more affluence. The toleration of the systematic moronization of children and adults alike by publicity and propaganda . . . fosters tolerance as a means for perpetuating the struggle for existence and suppressing the alternatives."9

Marcuse asserts that "the historical calculus of progress (which is actually the calculus of the prospective reduction of cruelty, misery, suppression) seems to involve the calculated choice between two forms of political violence: that on the part of the legally constituted powers . . . and that on the part of potentially subversive movements,"10 while the American society lacks real equality in rights, education, and property.

Political institutions serve to maintain the veneer of freedom while actually furthering oppression, and this situation cannot be improved by gradual changes to the system. "Under a system of constitutionally guaranteed and . . . practiced civil rights and liberties, opposition and dissent are tolerated unless they issue in violence and/or in exhortation to and organization of violent subversion. The underlying assumption is that the established society is free, and that any improvement, even a change in the social structure and social values, would come about in the normal course of events, prepared, defined, and tested in free and equal discussion, on the open marketplace of ideas and goods."11

People living in a "false consciousness" cannot change on their own. The people "must have access to authentic information; and . . . on this basis, their evaluation must be the result of autonomous thought."12 The truth is only seen by a minority of intellectuals, so it is their job to liberate the ignorant masses by reversing the tools and methods of the conservative-liberal world against the oppressors. "What we have in fact is government, representative government by a non-intellectual minority of politicians, generals, and businessmen. The record of this 'elite' is not very promising, and political prerogatives for the intelligentsia may not necessarily be worse for the society as a whole."[13] The new elite, the intelligentsia, is to show the way of liberation to the people by virtue of their intellectual superiority. "Who is to decide on the distinction between liberating and repressive . . . is not a matter of value-preference but of rational criteria."[14] Historically, "it seems that the violence emanating from the rebellion of the oppressed classes broke the historical continuum of injustice, cruelty, and silence for a brief moment, brief but explosive enough to achieve an increase in the scope of freedom and justice, and a better and more equitable distribution of misery and oppression in a new social system—in one word: progress in civilization."[15] "The English civil wars, the French Revolution, the Chinese and the Cuban Revolutions may illustrate the hypothesis. . . . True pacification requires the withdrawal of tolerance before the deed, at the stage of communication in word, print and picture."[16]

Marcuse "believe[s] that there is a 'natural right' of resistance for oppressed and overpowered minorities to use extralegal means if the legal ones have proved to be inadequate."[17] Marcuse suggests "the practice of discriminating tolerance in an inverse direction, as a means of shifting the balance between Right and Left by restraining the liberty of the Right, thus counteracting the pervasive inequality of freedom and strengthening the oppressed against the oppressors."[18]

The task is to take control of the system, institutions of authority, and hierarchies. "No government can be expected to foster its own subversion, but in a democracy such a right is vested in the people.... This means that the ways should not be blocked on which a subversive majority could develop, and if they are blocked by organized repression and indoctrination, their reopening may require apparently undemocratic means. They would include the withdrawal of toleration of speech and assembly from groups and movements which promote aggressive policies, armament, chauvinism, discrimination on the grounds of race and religion, or which oppose the extension of public services, social security, medical care, etc. Moreover, the restoration of freedom of thought may necessitate new and rigid restrictions on teachings and practices in the educational institutions."[19]

Freedom "can...under the prevailing conditions of tyranny by the majority, only be won in the sustained effort of radical minorities, willing to break this tyranny and to work for the emergence of a free and sovereign majority—minorities intolerant, militantly intolerant and disobedient to the rules of behavior which tolerate destruction and suppression."[20] In practice, this "could only be envisaged as results of large-scale pressure which would amount to an upheaval."[21] Should the oppressors resist, then their opponents may require apparently undemocratic means. "The exercise of civil rights by those who don't have them presupposes the withdrawal of civil rights from those who prevent their exercise.... Withdrawal of tolerance from regressive movements before they can become active; intolerance even toward thought, opinion, and word, and finally, intolerance in the opposite direction, that is, toward the self-styled conservatives, to the political Right."[22]

In the modern program of repression of the oppressors, the left-liberal/Marxist intelligentsia has not produced many new arguments since the days of Alinsky and Marcuse. Their followers today also believe that persons and social entities can be (de)constructed as an expression of the human will and *fiat*, and man can be perfected by sensitization or coercion. They are convinced that the transformation of human nature and a brighter future will open up perspectives in the history of humankind that cannot be hampered by past experiences, arguments, logic, requirements of consistency, or wisdom, nor by possible harmful effects or negative consequences. What has changed, however, is that Puritan-Jacobin-Marxist ideas have been integrated into mainstream American politics. The left-liberal intelligentsia and the Democratic Party are practically Marxist in their goals and methods. Today, partners in the Alinsky-Marcuse program include leaders of the "social" media technocracy, a significant proportion of the faculty and staff in universities, boards and centers of public education, a large part of the legal establishment, as well as violent statue-smashers and flashmobbers. They are also aided and abetted by certain self-serving Republican-conservative thinkers and organizations that continually offer concessions in a spirit of "live and let live."

THE BIBLICAL, CLASSICAL-LIBERAL, REPUBLICAN, CONSERVATIVE WORLDVIEW

The biblical, classical-liberal, republican, conservative worldview can be broadly summarized as follows: The ideals of freedom, equality before the law, and justice are manifested through persons, who, by taking responsibility for themselves and their environment, can contribute to the realization of social goals and ideals. Prosperity is based on individual efforts, so society must be built on merit. Excess and selfish individualism are harmful because certain goals can only be attained through cooperation, while individual well-being is ultimately also a function of the well-being of society as a whole. Collectivism is also seen as detrimental, with its idea that individuals should hand over control of their possessions to the public. They see the state as necessary wherever private efforts and resources are insufficient, and the checking of some dominant economic or other force may at times require the intervention of the republic. The success of the United States is seen in the fact that a wide range of people feel the system of ordered liberty as their own. Conservatives see human life as a civilizational continuum, in which it is the responsibility of the individual to preserve, enrich, and pass on an inherited culture. As Ronald Reagan put it in 1964, "Freedom is a fragile thing and it's never more than one generation away from extinction. It is not ours by way of inheritance; it must be fought for and defended constantly by each generation."[23] According to this view, America's history is a slow, imperfect, yet organic process of unfolding human freedom and prosperity.

Today's American Republican-Conservative camp, like conservative groupings worldwide, is diverse. But they are united in attempting to make decisions on the basis of the facts as they are, rather than by pursuing utopian dreams, and they prefer consensus and inclusive solutions to conflict. Beyond that, however, and in contrast to the era of "fusion conservatism" from 1980 to the 2010s, debates between conservative thinkers, think tanks, and generations, both in terms of content and methodology, have intensified.[24]

To help us understand the different perspectives, it may be useful to examine the mission statements of various prestigious conservative think tanks, including the leading intellectual institutions, The Heritage Foundation,[25] the classically liberal Cato Institute,[26] and the laissez-faire American Enterprise Institute.[27] The most common terms in the documents refer to individual political and economic freedom: individual freedom, equal opportunities, prosperity, free enterprise, the free market, traditional American values, and civil society. They are likewise unanimous in supporting a limited state, but with strong defense and peacekeeping capability. It appears that in the principal communications of the most prestigious conservative think tanks, the fundamental institution of Western—and indeed human—civilization, the family, is just an ancillary theme, not to be emphasized as part of the core mission. They appear to believe that individual freedom, a free market, and individual enterprise, together with a limited state, can ensure the survival of a good, just, and virtuous society and ordered liberty, via some invisible hand. In contrast, some conservative research institutes attach primary importance to the family as an institution that inculcates the virtues and capabilities that are necessary both for meaningful attachments and belongings, and for technical and material advancement from generation to generation. At the Center for Ethics and Public Policy, for example, the Economics and Ethics Program "aims to foster economic policies—in areas ranging from the tax code to retirement pensions to health care—that recognize and promote the family as the central social institution of American civilization."[28] According to the Core Principles of the Acton Institute, "Since persons are by nature social,

79

various human persons develop social institutions. The institutions of civil society, especially the family, are the primary sources of a society's moral culture."[29]

PROBLEMS AND SOLUTIONS FOR TODAY'S AMERICAN SOCIETY FROM A CONSERVATIVE AND LEFT-LIBERAL PERSPECTIVE

The views of left-liberals and conservatives differ not only with regard to principles, but also in their respective assessment of the significance of particular social facts and problems.

To assess what problems are of most concern for left-liberals, let's consider the statements of the Brookings Institution. Brookings considers itself impartial, yet provides the ideological, the public policy, and, to a significant extent, the staffing background of Democratic administrations. In his introduction to the 2021 Annual Report, President John R. Allen explains America's biggest problems: "[In the face of] a growing climate crisis, the appearance of new and deadly COVID variants, continued systemic racism throughout the country, and economic inequality that leaves far too many people behind .... [Brookings is working] toward a better, brighter future of peace and prosperity for all ... [with] a series of innovative, implementable federal policy ideas on racial justice, worker mobility, economic growth and dynamism, global governance, international security, climate resiliency, and more."[30]

There is a broad consensus among left-liberals that the state has a key role to play in solving problems, which is in line with their idea that persons, even with their (perceived) individual freedom, are unwilling or unable to recognize and solve social problems, and therefore, through state (federal) regulation they must be sensitized or forced to change. Such a view seems to miss the institution of the family, which connects individuals and the middle-class, and, more broadly, a society. It is instructive to see that Brookings recently shook off the notion of the family from the title of one of their prime programs:

> The Center for Economic Security and Opportunity was formerly known as the Center on Children and Families which focused on policies that affect the well-being of America's children and their parents, especially children in less advantaged families. The Center's name change reflects the evolution of its work and broader focus: ... first, fundamental needs through a robust safety net and good jobs, second, building skills through quality education, training, and opportunities for personal development, and third, strengthening capacities of families and communities through investment in the care economy, immigrant integration, and other social infrastructure.[31]

Such a change in emphasis raises difficulties in understanding the problems and potential solutions for issues such as the contraction of the American middle class.[32] Lacking an account of the family, the authors seem to remain perplexed about the causes of, and remedies for, this contraction.[33]

In addition to economic growth, conservatives are most preoccupied with demographic and cultural issues. These include the crisis within the institution of marriage, abortion, declining life expectancy, the issue of children born out of wedlock, the question of "social loneliness" which is worsening with the decline of religious practice, and the issue of mass culture and education becoming increasingly secularized. Conservatives are concerned about the weakening of attachments, and the spread of social anomie as a result of a less pronounced sense of belonging, as well as the increase in legal and illegal opioid use and crime, the disintegration of public order, especially in large cities, and the increasing number of suicides.[34] However, conservatives are far from unanimous with regard to the role that the state should play in supporting families, churches, and traditions, which are crucial for building a safety net, a sense of attachment, and belonging. The role of the state in the integration of legal immigrants to replace unborn Americans in the labor market, and in the fight against illegal immigration (border protection, national security) are topics of debate. Conservatives acknowledge the segregation of the meritocratic elite in terms of culture and lifestyle, and the decline of social mobility in general.[35] They respect the pursuit of knowledge, which since the Enlightenment has deservedly been esteemed, but are puzzled by the growing isolation between those with a tertiary education and those with a lower level of education who are engaged in physical work or health and medical, mental, or elderly care, and are often seen as losers.[36] Another problem in conservative eyes is the problem of income distribution between the state, corporate sector, and households, which is further complicated by considerations for racial and gender equality. Finally, conservatives see a problem in the positive legal imperialism that is stealthily undermining the authority of elected officials, and in woke linguistic authoritarianism, which is shattering the political community into ever smaller, resentful and envious, and more mutually hostile parts.

However American politicians and institutions rank the problems, the material-technical political machinery today is only prepared to manage socio-mechanical problems and reallocate (generated or borrowed) resources. It is no longer suitable for discussing national strategic issues. The work of Congress is mostly limited to struggles over the allocation of budgetary resources, as the rethinking of revenues and expenditures from a socio-philosophical standpoint runs into resistance from business lobbies and middle-class interest-groups who insist on their rights. For example, in the case of both Democratic and Republican governments, business groups defending their benefits have successfully prevented the simplification and normalization of tax laws. Due to the enactment of individual rebates and benefits, US tax law amounted to some 2,600 pages (1 million words) by 2014, up from 504 pages in 1939. Similarly, the Affordable Health Act (Obamacare), passed in 2009, came in the end to some 1,990 pages (235,000 words). By comparison, the King James Bible contains 788,000 words. Instead of clarifying national strategy issues, the political class deals with the distribution of resources based upon the pressures and directives advocated by an ever-increasing number of business, racial, gender, ideological, and other interest groups. Politicians have the narrow choice either of enacting unpopular tax increases, or of increasing public debt to the extent that they can get away with it in the eyes of the voters. The increase of public debt is based upon the "original sin" whereby, as we have seen, the discretionary part of the budget is financed entirely by increasing the public debt, a burden that will have to be borne by future generations. Instead of strategic debates, Congress is increasingly preoccupied with empty shadow-boxing and cultural battles.

A RETURN TO THE IDEALS OF
AN AMERICAN GENIUS

The United States was originally based upon the mutual acceptance of ideals and would quickly have collapsed if the system of virtues and traditions necessary for the integration of society had not been consolidated. In his farewell address, Washington argued that religion and morality were indispensable pillars of America's prosperity. It is a view that still has merit today. According to historical experience, the domain in which the capacities and virtues cited by Washington are passed on is the family, together with churches and educational institutions, and complemented by a state that embodies the larger community, the nation. However, the short-term, results-oriented American mindset that prevails today seems to be dominated by matters of material wealth creation and distribution. Conservatives are preoccupied with the free market and enterprise, while Democrats are preoccupied with the question of how to distribute wealth ever more evenly, as they believe this will make America successful and Americans happy, respectively. By contrast, the ancients whom America's Founding Fathers so esteemed, such as Socrates, maintained that "virtue does not come from money, but from virtue comes money and all other good things to man, both to the individual and to the state."[37] Summarizing his life experiences before his execution, Socrates argued that human good, including wealth, was a consequence of virtues, not the other way around. Socrates is here referring to the intellectual (arithmetic, logic, geometry) and moral (wisdom, moderation, justice, courage, generosity, self-sacrifice) virtues that form the basis of social order in the Western tradition. There is no doubt that wealth-generating economic activity, the free market, and enterprise all develop intellectual virtues and also certain moral virtues, such as intelligence and courage; but they are clearly neutral towards, or in stark contrast to, other moral virtues, such as moderation or sacrifice. Likewise, the idea of wealth equality is at best morally neutral, and at worst detrimental to moral virtues, for it is founded on envy, results in laziness, restrains ambitious and courageous people, and ultimately leads to tyranny and equal impoverishment for all.

The ideals that characterize the American genius can only be upheld by virtues inculcated within that most fundamental and influential form of social existence, the place of care, nurture, and education: the family.[38] It is here that person learns the rules and values of the community, as well as the chief virtues and all other human goods, whether public or private. In the family one learns about attachment,[39] respect, authority and hierarchy, what is good and evil, just and unjust, love, fairness, generativity, caring for others, and giving without recourse or exchange based on reciprocity. Family attachment is vital to a person's healthy physical, mental, and spiritual development. As James Heckman, a Nobel laureate in Economics in 2000, has shown, family upbringing and early childhood development play a key role in the development of the adult personality.[40] In the absence of childhood attachments, the individual may have difficulty developing meaningful interpersonal relationships and belonging to social entities in adulthood. There is no known technique that can reproduce and make a person fit for social coexistence outside the institution of the family.

Another space in which virtues and abilities may be passed on is the education system. However, since the 1960s, the education system has demonstrated a "utilitarianism (a carrier of metaphysical nihilism,

epistemological skepticism, and moral relativism)"
that led "to a 'dictatorship of relativism' in which
coercive state power was deployed to impose a rel-
ativistic 'ethic' on all of society."[41] Today, American educational institutions are abolishing the basic
principle of human discourse, which is to respect the
human dignity of one's interlocutor, and even force
students classified as descendants of oppressors to
endure humiliation because of the real or perceived
sins of their ancestors. There has also been an attack
on the previously accepted constitutional principle
that parents have a fundamental right, above and
beyond political considerations, to raise and educate
their children as they choose.[42]

A good starting point for rethinking the role of the
state in national strategy may be found, for instance,
in a proposal by the Acton Institute: "The institutions
of civil society, especially the family, are the primary
sources of a society's moral culture. These social institutions are neither created by nor derive their legitimacy
from the state. The state must respect their autonomy
and provide the support necessary to ensure the free
and orderly operation of all social institutions in their
respective spheres."[43] Without the family, neither "life,
liberty, and the pursuit of happiness," nor wealth, nor
social entities can survive.

Recent data indicates that while federal health,
retirement, homeland security, and military spending all continue to rise, the proportion of budgetary
resources spent on parenting and families is declining.
According to 2020 data, total federal, state, and local
government spending on those aged 0–18, who make
up 23 per cent of the population, was $18,000 per
person. At the same time, $40,000 per person (largely
retirement funding and health insurance) was spent on

those over the age of 65, who make up 17 per cent of the population. Child and family benefits come from two sources, with one third of total spending coming from the federal budget and two thirds from states and local authorities. The share of spending on families and education in the federal budget is declining relative to other areas. Federal expenditure related to the 0–18 age group still accounted for 10.7 per cent of the budget in 2010, but had decreased to 9.8 per cent by 2022, while military expenditure is 12 per cent, interest payments on government debt eight per cent, and expenditure for other purposes 31 per cent. In 2020, 33 per cent of federal spending went to retirement funding and health insurance benefits for the adult population, and 7.4 per cent was spent on children. Sixty per cent of federal spending on children goes to those from a low-income background, while 30 per cent concerns tax incentives and rebates that encourage both childbearing and working, and the remaining 10 per cent is paid out in a single lump sum per child.[44]

From all of this, it appears that America's political class does not recognize or value the role of the family and childcare institutions as key players in the transfer of skills and virtues.

The question for the coming years is whether Democrats and Republicans will be able to reach beyond their respective ideologies and business interests to rediscover and improve the operating conditions of strategic national institutions, including the family, education, and churches, to ensure the survival of the United States.

൭ℌ൦

American alternatives

I N THIS BOOK, WE HAVE BRIEFLY
looked at the genesis and the "theological" metaphors of the characteristic ideals that underpin
the American genius, such as freedom, equality before
the law, and justice in the history of the American
federation. We have seen that these ideals are often
contradicted in practice, and that a degree of cognitive
dissonance is often employed to rationalize injustices
committed. We have noted that America's political
and economic system has enjoyed unparalleled success in using the resources at its disposal to create
the most exceptional and dynamic material-technical
civilization in world history. We sought to form an
unbiased assessment of American history, taking into
account the historical logic of force used to ensure
preservation and growth of social entities, the moral
judgment of the methods used in the process, and the
necessity of considering an ultimate judgment before
some divine measure. In assessing the current state
of the American genius, we have covered the evolving
ideas of the American elite regarding the nature of
that genius, the future of the United States, and the
methods for proceeding. We have pointed out that it
is in the strategic national interest of Americans to
rethink the role of the family, school, church, and state
in passing on vital abilities and virtues fundamental
for good life in a unity of order.

We cannot know whether the American political system and elite will be able to debate and deliver in that direction, rather than merely engaging in games of resource allocation and culture wars. The American genius is an intellectual phenomenon, the future potential of which depends on the intent and capability of particular authentic persons and leaders. The future of the American genius depends on the ability of the elite to comprehend the desired human goods and unity of order in a changing world and to mobilize organizational capabilities to attend and preserve them. It is more than just administering affairs; it is an intentional drive to pass on the spiritual heritage of the American genius to the next generation. Given the mutual antagonism that characterizes relations between the Republican-conservative and left-liberal/Marxist camps today, it is reasonable to ask whether any personalities will eventually measure up to the challenge.

The fact that neither the left-liberal/Marxist nor the Republican-conservative camp seem to be strong enough to achieve a lasting dominant position in public politics makes it more likely that tensions will rise rather than dissipate. The deep divisions mean that, of the conflict resolution methods mentioned in the introduction, there seems little chance of the first—friendly cooperation between the camps—as the ideals of the two parties are fundamentally different. The second conflict resolution method is co-existence. Indeed, we are witnessing a legal and cultural cold war between camps living in parallel intellectual and geographical worlds, in bubbles, and the relative peace is due in part to the fact that the two groups still have enough intellectual and physical room to retreat and avoid open conflict. The third alternative—that the existential struggle of the two camps should lead to

open violence—seems unthinkable, given the relatively
even balance of power at the moment.

Still, there has already been one example in American history of open internal warfare fought by regular forces: the Civil War of 1861–65. The Civil War
was preceded by a protracted cold war, culminating in
the secession of the Southern states from the Union
(1860–61) and the establishment of the Confederacy.

Doubts were raised from the outset about the via-
bility of the United States as a federal state. Perceiving
this, George Washington, resigning from the presidency,
argued at length in his farewell speech that federalism
was in the overwhelming financial and political interests
of US citizens and states, as it provided security, unparalleled strength, and resources against external enemies,
while at the same time it would "avoid the necessity of
those overgrown military establishments which, under
any form of government, are inauspicious to liberty,
avoiding the need for overdeveloped military institutions
that are fatal to freedom under any form of government."[1]
However, he warned that while it was unrealistic to
imagine that states might attack each other in the absence
of a standing army, external alliances, attachments, and
intrigues could still stir up strife between them. Still, the
Union was to be seen as the mainstay of freedom, meaning that the love of freedom would make it desirable to
maintain that Union. Pondering the unity of order that
bound the United States in 1831, Tocqueville pointed
to perhaps the most sensitive aspect in the American
system, the danger of misinterpreting the ideals of its
founding and twisting their essence:

> The states formed the confederation of their own
> free will. In uniting, they did not forfeit their nation-
> ality and did not merge into a single people .... The
> present Union will survive only as long as all of its

member states continue to want to be part of it ....
The question is no longer whether the presently
confederated states might be able to separate but
whether they will wish to remain united.[2] ... The
Union can die in two ways: one of the confederated states may wish to ... break the common bond
in a violent way.... Or the federal government
may gradually lose its power if for some reason all
the united republics simultaneously reclaim their
independence.[3] ... When people recognize that the
weakness of the federal government is compromising
the existence of the Union, I have no doubt that
a reaction will take place in favor of force .... As
long as it is not attacked indirectly through interpretation of its laws, and as long as its substance
is not profoundly corrupted, a change of opinion,
internal crisis, or war could promptly restore the
vigor it needs.[4] ... Nevertheless, the future of the
republic should not be confused with the future
of the Union.

The Union is an accident, which will survive
only as long as circumstances allow, but the republic
seems to me the natural state of the Americans ....
The Union exists primarily in the law that created
it.[5] ... Obviously, only a long series of circumstances
all tending in the same direction could replace this
combination of laws, opinions, and mores with a
contrary one. If republican principles are to perish
in America, they will succumb only after a long,
frequently interrupted, repeatedly renewed period
of social travail.[6]

Today, it seems that the very ideals cherished by
the Founding Fathers, the ideals of freedom, equality
before the law, and justice, are being twisted, and
conservatives are on the defensive against left-liberal/
Marxist radicals in America (and in Europe). And
not even the Marxist radicals themselves can stop

the process, just as Robespierre, who initiated the execution of Danton, could not restrain his devotees from killing himself and Saint-Just during the terror of the French Revolution.

The existential threat which, as we have observed, confronts the American genius and the American way of life, as well as home, family, and privacy, will not end. Conservatives have made so many concessions to radical Marxists that they have little remaining lee-way to give further ground without abandoning their very identity. Conservative strategies which worked in ancient times—retreating to a clearing in the wil-derness, hiding in a monastery or a wine cellar, or perhaps establishing some sort of conservative res-ervation—will no longer suffice. The individualist strategy is a dead end, a form of self-abandonment. Only political association provides room to maneuver for the next generation, but associations require com-panions, family, friends, and fellow citizens to act in a hardworking, organized way. Without friends and family one cannot aspire to preserve a life worth living. The American genius can only exert its effect through the activities of flesh and blood people and leaders. Experience shows that a competent, moral leader can dynamize and make a weak organization successful, while a corrupt and incompetent one can destroy a functioning organization in a short time.

The escalation of conflicts could reach a point at which conservatives who believe in the ideals that characterize the American genius, and left-liberal Marx-ists who promote equality of consumption, wealth, and outcomes in general, will no longer be able to live together. John Courtney Murray warned of this possibility as early as 1960: "The disintegration may have begun a long time ago, and will one day happen.

Maybe one day the noble castle of democracy will be demolished, and when converted to the level of the majority principle, it will no longer be a castle, but a barn, or perhaps a mere hovel, where the weapons of tyranny will be kept."[7]

Disintegration may mean that certain states will secede from the Union. It may mean a process whereby, under Article V of the Constitution, the legislatures of two-thirds of the states initiate the convening of a constitutional assembly, the decisions of which take effect after the approval of three-quarters of the states. In fact, in the event of a split, it would become apparent whether the lifeworld and unity of order offered by the conservative American genius or the left-liberal/ Marxist approach could better sustain the human goods of their citizens.

We do not know what the future holds. Still, we cannot live without ideals. American conservatives are close to experiencing John Winthrop's 1630 prophecy: "If we shall deal falsely with our God in this work we have undertaken, and so cause Him to withdraw His present help from us, we shall be made a story and a by-word through the world."[8]

Leo Strauss formulated Winthrop's warning in the broadest "theological-political" context in 1953, arguing that "man cannot live without light, guidance, knowledge; only through knowledge of the good can he find the good that he needs. The fundamental question, therefore, is whether men can acquire that knowledge of the good without which they cannot guide their lives individually or collectively by the unaided efforts of their natural powers, or whether they are dependent for that knowledge on Divine Revelation. No alternative is more fundamental than this: human guidance or divine guidance."[9]

After all, reaching certainty is impossible. What is left is the eternal quest for good human life in a unity of order, as Alasdair MacIntyre maintained: "We have then arrived at a provisional conclusion about the good life for man: the good life for man is the life spent in seeking for the good life for man, and the virtues necessary for the seeking are those which will enable us to understand what more and what else the good life for man is."[10]

One thing is certain. Without the ideals of the American genius—freedom, equality before the law, and justice—the world would be worse off. The success of the American attempt at ordered liberty is vital, not just for Americans, but for all of us around the world.

We should stay hopeful, as our time "too is a time of waiting for new and unpredictable possibilities of renewal. It is also a time for resisting as prudently and courageously and justly and temperately as possible the dominant social, economic, and political order of advanced modernity. So it was twenty-six years ago [1981], so it is still [2007]"[11] and, we can add, so it is in 2024.

We should keep an eye on America!

AFTERWORD
By George Friedman

I ENCOUNTERED JÁNOS CSÁK LONG before I met him. He is a Hungarian steeped in America, awed by it, and doubting it. I am Hungarian-born, but lived my life as an American. Hungarian life is unique, as is life in all nations, but more so. As a Hungarian scientist once said, while explaining why Hungarians excel in so many scientific areas, "We are from Mars." They may well come from there, but having arrived from Mars, many left Hungary for America. A Hungarian seeking to understand America is, in a way, routine. My family had to do it over and over. America is not a declarative sentence. Thus, János's search to understand America from a Hungarian standpoint, far from appearing idiosyncratic, strikes me as a most reasonable thing.

János is fluent in American moral history. He and I read the same books and wondered at the possibilities embedded in the *Federalist Papers*, the reality that suffused Tocqueville. We saw the virtue in America's beauty and flaws. We crossed paths late in our lives. Perhaps it was best we didn't meet earlier. Youth does not allow for subtlety; it demands certainty. By the time we met, we understood that absolute revelation still needs to be explicated, understood, and wondered at, and that lives lived in certainty were monstrous. János is a Hungarian patriot to his soul. Hungary is for me a recollection of family, and its explication is drawn from the subtlety of an American dinner table. I am an American patriot in the manner in which Americans live. This is my country, and here I stand.

There is a painting by Rembrandt entitled "Aristotle Contemplating a Bust of Homer." Aristotle, clad in the golden cords that bound him to his state, looks longingly at Homer, the author of truth and beauty. He wishes to give up his life, a life of the relentless demand of the political, but he will not. But still he gazes. And this makes him my brother, for neither of us can abandon the chains and submerge ourselves in beauty—except at rare moments of recklessness, for we both know the terrible risks in this world, and in our countries, of being seduced by the beautiful at the cost of the necessary.

János has written a superb book which judges my country by both its virtues and vices. His intention perhaps is to infuse his country with the virtues of mine, but he would purify it of our vices. He knows as I do that vice and virtue, in their dangerous and subtle ways, cannot be separated and that neither of our countries could live without both. His country collaborated with Hitler's Germany. Those not facing Aristotle squarely would not see that the choice was not between good and evil, but between many evils which Hungary did not survive, and from which it will never quite recover. My own country has its own sins—the sin of slavery is but one. The question is whether America would have survived without slavery, or whether it deserved to survive. Yes, others were deeply involved—the Dutch, the Portuguese, the African kings themselves—but we speak here of beloved countries, and we have subtle explanations, not necessarily true ones. Each of our conversations appear to be about *Realpolitik*. They are all about the relationship of sin and our countries, in which each of us is part of both, he by choice, I by birth.

János's love of America is, I think, his understanding that his Europe comprises both victims and

victimizers over recent centuries that neither Homer
nor Aristotle could embrace. Europe has become an
intermittent charnel house, and his Hungary is trapped
in it. He finds in the document that founded the American republic a moral virtue he envies. He also sees
great vice. But while there is constant vice throughout
the world, the virtues of the American founding, its
intent and clarity, are not just American, but something
human and beautiful. Two questions must be asked.
First, can America survive its vices while asserting
the truth (the vices were not American; they were
human, and vices cloud us all)? The second question
is whether a nation so conceived can long endure. The
problem is that he is speaking about a country close to
his life philosophically, morally and institutionally. But
as someone who was given refuge in America, I grew
up a poor outsider, yet was permitted and encouraged
to live an idiosyncratic life.

János says that the United States is divided in
unprecedented ways. The United States fought a revolution in which Americans themselves were deeply
and at times viciously divided. The Civil War sav-
aged the country. The rage toward the United States
between classes during the Great Depression made
many authors and Europeans say that America's best
days were harming it.

I live in a rural area of Texas, divided among Anglos
and Hondurans. Any outsider would see us as hope-
lessly divided, and each faction makes clear that the
other is ruining America. Yet we live next to each
other and work together, Trump voters and Biden
voters, without discord. There are some here who are
intrusive on both sides, but they are generally shunned.
The media looks at America as if it were a country
foreign to them, and it is easy to think that the country

is raging. After all, we raged in the American Revolution and Civil War and the Great Depression. But
Americans see the world in very different ways, and
see it without needing to, or being able to, express it.

The truth is that Americans, for the most part, rarely
care about politics. The idea of Europeans, that politics
is the center of their lives' gravity, does not hold here.
The obsession here is work and money, and since there
can never be enough money coming in, this is where
anguish and rage enters. Some worry deeply or casually
about gender; others do not care at all. What they live
for is money, so their politics is money.

This focus is due to the principles of the founding.
Government was given little power and fewer resources.
It was there to wage war against foreign nations, not to
run the economy. The making of money was a private
undertaking. Although in time the nation, and thus the
government, grew, growth intruded upon the elegant
vision the founders crafted.

Americans care about money and the kind of life
it can buy. When the economy fails, then America
rises. János speaks of this. But like many Americans,
he mistakes the routine for the catastrophic. America's well-being rests on the destruction of inefficient
businesses that degrade wealth. It is easy to start a
business, but much harder to destroy a parasitic one.
Most businessmen cling too long and lose money in
a hopeless cause. The same can be said for governments. America's success lies in its social and economic
ruthlessness, killing any business that underperforms.
What to a Hungarian might look like the end of America is instead the foundation of American prosperity.

There is a difference in America that defines us.
When my family arrived in the Bronx, a charity provided us with an apartment and a small sum of money,

and left us to survive or drown. My father found a job in two days, so we ate. In time, we ate well. The kindness of America is that at its best it is a land without mercy, where you are free to succeed or fail based on your will. In this sense, what is terrible for a Hungarian to see in America is, for me, the thing that Europe lacks. There is kindness where there should be ruthlessness.

Where János and I find common ground is in the respective foundings, public morals, and obligations of our countries. We meet as friends do, to argue and grow wiser. Hidden in all of this book are two questions. One is Abraham Lincoln's: Can a nation so conceived long endure? The second is whether a nation crafted from the best thoughts of the Enlightenment can fail to disappoint? And can János, who loved the Enlightenment as Thomas Jefferson did, bear the sense of betrayal that the great experiment is now in the hands of humans?

János brings us to the writings and words of the founders. One of the extraordinary things about America is that few nations in human history were consciously forged with a moral purpose. The founders—János explicates from their work far better than I can—sought a society where the individual was not the servant or slave of their betters, but an autonomous being, living freely. It was a radical and difficult path to take, for how can a human be alone and survive? To solve this problem, they created a regime that would control the nation by having an equal voice in which it governs through a selection of governors. There would be no born aristocracy. Nor was there to be a state religion. They wanted a nation that was free and was governed as such. In all the writing of the founders, it boiled down to this, and to one other thing: what you earn is yours, no lords would take a piece, and aside from taxes, no nation would lay claim to the sweat of your brow. The complex tomes contain far more than this, of course, but this was their essence.

America is a moral project that struggles with the relationship between secularism and war. When war was declared, as it would be and as it always is, soldiers fought for their own country, and not for a prince. This was the intent, and the question is whether the intent and effort outweighed our sins.

The truth of the United States was the balance of power between federal and state governments. That is a deep truth. But there was another truth, the truth that we came to America out of fear and arrived filled with fear. The institutional and moral sense is central to America. But fear was for centuries a founding principle. When Benjamin Franklin was asked what kind of government he and his had delivered to Americans, his answer was, "A republic, if you can keep it." It was moral because life was promised in the founding, moral because you were obligated to feed your family, and moral because you had a moral right to the fruits of your labor. The English spoke of life, liberty and property; this was not Europe, where a lord protected you for half your wealth.

The right to property was embedded in the founding of America. It could only be achieved with the brute strength of the individual. Having a gun made it possible to assert the right. What is important here is that in America, as in other nations, the moral imperatives were shaped by fear and necessity. The nature of the American army, in the beginning, was that each soldier should bring his own weapons. This has shaped America in ways that may be outmoded, and is certainly looked on uneasily by some Americans, but it is as difficult to change as would be freedom of speech.

It is here that, while not disagreeing with what János has written, I see another dimension, sacred to the American memory. America was founded, generation after generation, on fear. All Americans know this fear, though it subsides over the generations. It is rooted in Europe and defines America. I know of it because I was born a European and became an American. The charm of America is that it is possible to be seen by other Americans as being American within a fraction of a generation. This soothes fear and loss, but does not alleviate them altogether. But without understanding this, it is impossible to understand the pain that is linked to America's beauty.

America is a nation built by strangers. For the first two centuries, the strangers came from Europe and Africa, but only the Europeans chose to come here. They did not come alone. They brought their wives and children, leaving behind all that they had known, and knowing that the kisses exchanged with those left behind were likely the last ever. Such a journey marked the beginning of American history, when the Pilgrims left Europe haunted by death and danger. They came to America because their lives were bitter and anguished in Europe. I was, as I have said, born a Hungarian, but Hungary had come to be seen as a place of death and danger by my parents. Both had been taken from their homes by the Germans and sent to concentration camps. When they returned after the war, they were overjoyed to be home. Then the Soviets came and prepared their lists of enemies, which included my father. The family fled not because of Hungary but because Hungary was weak and could not stop monsters from ruling it (a European story in itself). America welcomed us as it had all immigrants, first with an open door, and then with a complete indifference to their fate. But for their children, the possibilities were endless.

Along with the *Federalist Papers*, this is what America is. You flee the place you fear for America, which then subjects you to the fearsome trial of indifference, forcing you to be strong and to fight to survive and thrive. The children never quite forget the tale, or at least they romanticize the anger and sense of loss with forgetfulness. America imposed this price on all who came. My father found a job in a country where you could lose a job quickly if you were not strong. He lived in fear of that, and of not being able to support and protect his family.

It did not plan this, but America was built by immigrants, people who were lost when they came, and its indifference imposed an ordeal that crushed the weak but made all things possible to those who were supple and strong. Fear and poverty caused them to leave Europe, and more recently Asian countries, and they were met by the same challenges of fear and poverty. America broke some, but of the rest it built the robust families who have long memories, and the fear that drove them and received them gave way to the hunger of the old country, the one our parents clung to. I did not speak English until I entered school. Our family spoke only Hungarian at home. The vague sense of the motherland persists. And it is at first a terrible burden, later a subtle confusion.

America was a European creation. It grew not out of European culture but out of Europe's ability to instill fear, to compel generations to flee. I exclude Africans, of course, because their nightmare was more profound and lasting, and because János is dealing with the soul of America. The Africans were denied entry to America for so long that their suffering is unique, even if the American crime of slavery was far more complex and shared profoundly with others in our world.

The land was generous, the country was not. It sought to starve you and to twist your life. To a great extent, this is missing or superficially dealt with in the documents and genuinely brilliant books that were written. But as we understand the republic that Benjamin Franklin and his colleagues gave us, we must remember the pain that brought the settlers to the country and forced them to give the last morsel of their strength. Americans live by fear, strength, and more often than not, triumph. Many things made America unique, not least of which was, along with its form of government and moral state, the fact that it was possible and even common to triumph in ordinary life.

When I attended university and studied the US through the prism of political philosophy, the idea of fear, hunger and triumph meant little. To me, it was the thing that was always missing, the thing my father and Hungary drove into me. János's treatment of the American regime provides a powerful vision of what America was and became. It was also a land with little pity, requiring a powerful hand that lost its fear.

America presents itself as the land of the free and the home of the brave. But America is far more complex than its national anthem suggests. Americans came into being afraid, and their fear forced them to be brave and compelled them to be free. Those things were the engine that drove them to shape their lives with an emphatic love of freedom, and that aligned them with the founders' vision. The words to the national anthem were written by Francis Scott Key during the War of 1812. There was fear in that conflict, of course, but bravery and freedom were topmost in the minds of Americans. Freedom meant freedom from Britain, and from any rule outside America. It was over a century later that Congress adopted that song in 1931 as its national anthem. By then, America had gone through the Civil War and World War I. Americans feared death less than they feared the loss of freedom.

János shows us the dynamic the founders imagined guiding America to greatness. It was a greatness built on the individual confronting the frightening wilderness, the frightening strangers, and the Europeans that gave birth to them and now stalked the nation, hoping to create a nation in their own image and punish those who would rebel. The English, French, Spaniards, and others came for American riches and were all remembered with fear by the Americans, and that fear gave rise to the bravery of defeating them.

I must also address the sins of slavery and the Indians. Slavery was introduced to America by Europeans. The first slaves were carried on a Dutch Ship that traded its slaves for goods in the first colony, Jamestown. The slave trade was a European tale. Ships from England, the Netherlands and Portugal travelled to West Africa and traded with leaders of African tribes. The Europeans rarely captured slaves on the run, but the slavers had regular business relations. The United States is frequently and reasonably condemned for slavery, but an interesting point is that the largest slaveholders were the Portuguese, not the Americans. The Portuguese, in league with other nations at various times, dominated Brazil with African slaves far in excess of the number in America and continued the practice of slavery a generation longer than Americans.

Other European nations did not use African slaves, but practiced the equivalent of slavery with serfs.

However, they did sell and trade in African slaves, because they practiced entangling their own country-men in the role of slaves, born to lead a life of service to their betters. The Americans are in no way excused from the guilt of slavery, but the story is more complex than Europeans consider it, blind as they all are to their own guilt, although it is true that American guilt is far greater. And yet slavery was not abolished in the British empire until 1837, thirty years before the Americans fought a brutal war against slavery and abolished it. The British were very thoughtful. They paid the owners for the slaves freed but not the freed slaves.

The tale of the Indians is far more complex than most know. North America is a vast continent, and it was first populated by many nations trivialized as "tribes"—and savage at that. These nations made constant war on each other, just as Europeans are wont to do. When the French arrived in Canada, they found a coalition of five nations, the most powerful being the Iroquois, waging war against another power. The French were trapping beavers to sell for hats on the European market. The Iroquois offered the French an alliance against the Mohawks, who dominated the area where the beavers lived. When this happened, the Mohawks faced disaster. They reached out to the English for an alliance to save themselves. It was much like Europe; the English and French were at war globally, and in Canada they entered an alliance with other nations to secure their interest and to betray less powerful nations.

When the Americans moved westward, they encountered many nations that would ally with them. The reason was the fear of a powerful empire, known as the Comanche, that spread out of the Rockies east-ward and conquered North America to Texas. There are admiring songs sung about the Comanche, but in the end they lost. But they were not annihilated. The Americans could be brutal and unprincipled in victory, but the story of the Indians was not one of systematic annihilation. The Americans behaved as Europeans had for centuries. And this was their sin. America had been founded to be free of Europe's brutality. But in waging wars with Indian nations they were no better.

One of the things that charms me about my country is that, after struggles, we accept that the guilt falls on all of us. Unlike Germans, who think that time generates distance, Americans on the whole accept the responsibility, and the struggles over racism and Indian rights are battles that are waged in America by Americans. Few other countries choose to bear that burden.

To understand Americans today, it must be remembered that we are afraid. We are afraid of foreign threats, domestic threats, economic threats, and imagined threats. The world we left and the world we built here have the same force of fear. But this fear does not paralyze. The writing of Tocqueville touches on this theme, which is that, where fear and paralysis are the norm, fear and action are the American norm. Sometimes the fear is justified, sometimes not. Sometimes it is magnified, and sometimes Americans feel helpless. But the fundamental truth of America is that fear galvanizes Americans. It creates the land of the free and the home of the brave. Many times Americans respond through marshaling excessive and imprudent force, but sometimes by saving the Republic from phantoms and other times from the horrors of the world.

The founders knew of war; they went to war with the vastly more powerful British military. The founding documents created the framework that harnessed the fear, and fought the British to surrender. Had that not happened, the documents that founded our understanding of ourselves as a nation would have been irrelevant. That the documents described not only the rights but the duties of an American made it possible to make the case for independence, plan the war, and call men to arms.

What is most striking is what emerged from the war: a regime that was envisioned by the founders and embodied in the Constitution, a regime unique in that it balanced obligations and rights, and understood the nature of the human condition. Where other nations envisioned fear as betrayal, the founders saw fear as a shaping power in the American spirit, and shaped it with prudence at the heart of the founding.

America was born in the beautiful and symmetric logic and understanding that János has presented to us, a presentation that grasps the extraordinary nature of the regime. My minor addition is that the Constitution was born in battle as well as reason. And that it was the relationship between fear and greatness that allowed wisdom to be hallowed.

The fundamental tension in America is the tension between the founding and its documents, and the reality Americans experienced when they left Europe to occupy America. There was great decency and great hypocrisy in the founding, but it was not as absolute as might be thought. The Indians were treated ruthlessly, in the European fashion. I always wonder what happened to the residents of the Carpathian Basin that today's Hungarians occupy. I look at the European occupation of Africa and wonder whether guilt is called for or felt.

Applying morality to history is a tricky business. János and I have lived different lives in different papers. But one thing makes us brothers: We are both awed by the moral and political vision of the American founders, and the degree to which that vision has become real.

America is a land of crisis. It surges recklessly, retreats in disorder and gives the rest of the world the belief that America is a catastrophe, especially when the government flounders as it was designed to do. My country invented itself and continues to invent itself. It is not the government that does this, for the founders did not give it the power to shape America, nor do politicians have the imagination. As America reaches the exhaustion of an era, a new era emerges from the ashes of the old. Politically, economically and technologically, this is a harrowing trip. But it is also a trip filled with rage and exhilaration. We the people have built a more perfect union, as Tocqueville antici-pated, and one that Europeans through the centuries saw as failure while surging onto our teeming shores. János understands this far better than most Europeans.

We all lead sinful lives, and so do nations. But I stand with János in his admiration of the American founding. That it achieved less than it wants to speaks to the human condition. We all attain less than we would hope. But the founders' hopes towered where the hopes of others were meager. So they failed to achieve their goal. They still stand above other nations in what they built from nothing. János is deeply impressed with what America has achieved. I live in the country our founders created, whose principle is theirs—my duty is to do more than I thought and blame no one for my failures, and allow no one to claim my success. And I stand by my country in battle or in speech. In this János and I are joined in our admiration of America and in our sentiment toward Hungary.

ENDNOTES

NOTES TO FOREWORD

1 Harvey C. Mansfield and Delba Winthrop, "Editors' Introduction," in Alexis de Tocqueville, *Democracy in America*, trans. Harvey C. Mansfield and Delba Winthrop (Chicago: University of Chicago Press, 2000), xvii.

2 An insightful collection of essays about a number of these authors is found in *America Through European Eyes: British and French Reflections on the New World from the Eighteenth Century to the Present*, ed. Aurelian Craiutu and Jeffrey C. Isaac (University Park, PA: The Pennsylvania State University Press, 2009), which includes my essay, "What G. K. Chesterton Saw in America: The Cosmopolitan Threat from a Patriotic Nation," ch. 10. See also James L. Nolan, Jr., *What They Saw in America: Alexis de Tocqueville, Max Weber, G. K. Chesterton, and Sayyid Qutb* (New York: Cambridge University Press, 2016).

3 Tocqueville, *Democracy in America*, op. cit., Vol. 1, Part 1, Ch. 2, p. 42.

4 Eric Voegelin, *The New Science of Politics: An Introduction* (Chicago: University of Chicago Press, 1987); Leo Strauss, *Natural Right and History* (Chicago: University of Chicago Press, 1965).

NOTES TO INTRODUCTION

1 Pierre Manent, "Does French Culture have a Future?" *First Things*, August 1, 2016; https://www.firstthings.com/web-exclusives/2016/08/does-french-culture-have-a-future, accessed November 25, 2023.

2 George Friedman, *The Storm Before the Calm* (New York: Doubleday, 2020), 2, 5.

3 Paul Johnson, *A History of the American People* (New York: Weidenfeld & Nicolson, 1997), 4.

NOTES TO CHAPTER ONE

1 Russell Kirk, *The Roots of American Order* (Wilmington: ISI, 2003 [1974]).

2 John D. Mueller, *Redeeming Economics: Rediscovering the Missing Element* (Wilmington, Delaware: ISI Books, Paperback Edition, 2014), 26–34, 73–75.

3 John Stuart Mill, *On Liberty*, in John Stuart Mill, *On Liberty and Utilitarianism* (Longman, Green, Longman, Roberts & Green, 1864), 22.

4 John Winthrop, *A Model of Christian Charity* [1630] (Boston: Collections of the Massachusetts Historical Society, 1838), https://history.hanover.edu/texts/winthmod.html, accessed November 25, 2023.

5 Quoted from Samuel Goldman, *After Nationalism: Being in an Age of Division* (Philadelphia: University of Pennsylvania Press, 2021), 19.

6 Benjamin Franklin, *Observations Concerning the Increase of Mankind* (1751), points 6 and 8, https://founders.archives.gov/documents/Franklin/01-04-02-0080, accessed November 25, 2023.

7 Aristotle, *Politics*, 1295b. http://www.perseus.tufts.edu/hopper/text?doc=Perseus%3Atext%3A1999.01.0058%3Abook%3D4%3Asection%3D1295b, accessed January 15, 2024.

8 R. E. Brown, *Middle-Class Democracy and the Revolution in Massachusetts, 1691–1780* (Ithaca, NY: Cornell University Press, 1955).

9 Alexis de Tocqueville, *Democracy in America* (NY: The Literary Classics of the United States, 2004), 50–51.

10 Quoted from Goldman, *After Nationalism*, 26.

11 See for example, Marbury v. Madison (1803), National Archives, https://www.archives.gov/milestone-documents/marbury-v-madison, accessed November 25, 2023.

12 Aristotle, *Politics*, 1279a–b. http://www.perseus.tufts.edu/hopper/text?doc=Perseus%3Atext%3A1999.01.0058%3Abook%3D3%3Asection%3D1279b, accessed January 15, 2024.

13 South Carolina Ordinance Of Nullification, November 24, 1832, https://avalon.law.yale.edu/19th_century/ordnull.asp, accessed January 14, 2024.

14 Quoted from Alexis de Tocqueville, op. cit., 814.

15 The Declaration of Independence of the People of the United States, July 4, 1776, https://www.archives.gov/founding-docs/declaration-transcript, accessed January 15, 2024.

NOTES TO CHAPTER TWO

1 John Jay, *The charge of Chief Justice Jay, to the grand inquest of the county of Ulster, on the ninth day of September 1777*, https://founders.archives.gov/documents/Jay/01-01-02-0275. Accessed January 14, 2024.

2 *The Papers of Alexander Hamilton*, vol. 1, *1768–1778*, ed.

Harold C. Syrett (New York: Columbia University Press, 1961), 81–165.

3   The Declaration of Independence of the People of the United States, July 4, 1776, https://www.archives.gov/founding-docs/declaration-transcript, accessed January 15, 2024.

4   Ibid.

5   Tocqueville, 803–4.

6   Aristotle, *Nicomachean Ethics*, 1170b. http://www.perseus.tufts.edu/hopper/text?doc=Perseus%3Atext%3A1999.01.0054%3Abekker+page%3D1170b%3Abekker+line%3D1, accessed January 15, 2024.

7   Tocqueville, 160.

8   George Washington, "First Inaugural Address," April 30, 1789, https://avalon.law.yale.edu/18th_century/wash1.asp, accessed December 8, 2023.

9   George Washington, "Farewell address," September 19, 1796. https://avalon.law.yale.edu/18th_century/washing.asp, accessed December 8, 2023.

10   Tocqueville, 34–35.

11   Tocqueville, 560.

12   Tocqueville, 286.

13   Max Weber, *The Protestant Ethic and the Spirit of Capitalism* (London: George Allen & Unwin Ltd., 1930), 182.

14   Tocqueville, 287.

15   John Bodnar, *The Transplanted* (Bloomington: Indiana University Press, 1985), 169.

16   John O'Sullivan, "Annexation," *The United States Democratic Review*, Vol. XVII. 17, 1845, 5–10. https://books.google.hu/books?id=iJtFAQAAMAAJ&printsec=frontcover&redir_esc=y#v=onepage&q&f=false, accessed January 15, 2024.

17   G. W. F. Hegel, *The Phenomenology of Spirit* (Oxford University Press, 2018 [1807]).

18   Woodrow Wilson, "Request for Declaration of War on Germany, Washington, DC, April 2, 1917," https://millercenter.org/the-presidency/presidential-speeches/april-2-1917-address-congress-requesting-declaration-war, accessed November 25, 2023.

19   Woodrow Wilson, "Speech on the Fourteen Points," January 8, 1918, https://millercenter.org/the-presidency/presidential-speeches/january-8-1918-wilsons-fourteen-points, accessed November 25, 2023.

20   William Tyler Page, "The American's Creed," https://www.ushistory.org/DOCUMENTS/creed.htm, accessed November 25, 2023.

NOTES TO CHAPTER THREE

1 Maddison Project Database (MPD) 2020, https://www.rug.
nl/ggdc/historicaldevelopment/maddison/, accessed November
25, 2023.

2 United States Census Bureau, https://www.census.gov/pop-
clock/, accessed November 25, 2023.

3 The World Bank, https://data.worldbank.org/indicator/SP.
DYN.TFRT.IN?locations=US, accessed November 22, 2023.

4 CDC, "National Vital Statistics Reports," 72, No. 1, January
31, 2023, https://www.cdc.gov/nchs/data/nvsr/nvsr72/nvsr72-
01.pdf, accessed December 27, 2023.

5 Bryan Baker, Sarah Miller, "Estimates of the Lawful Permanent Resident Population in the United States and the Sub-
population Eligible to Naturalize: 2022," US Department of
Homeland Security, https://www.dhs.gov/sites/default/files/2022-
10/2022_0920_plcy_lawful_permenent_resident_population_esti-
mate_2022_0.pdf, accessed November 25, 2023.

6 Bryan Baker, "Estimates of the Illegal Alien Population
Residing in the United States: January 2015," US Department
of Homeland Security, https://www.dhs.gov/sites/default/files/
publications/18_1214_PLCY_pops-est-report.pdf, accessed November 25, 2023; Bryan Baker, "Estimates of the Unauthorized
Immigrant Population Residing in the United States: January
2015–January 2018," US Department of Homeland Security,
http://tinyurl.com/4nhv62ju, accessed: December 27, 2023.

7 "Foreign Born: 2019 Current Population Survey Detailed
Tables," https://www.census.gov/data/tables/2021/demo/foreign-
born/cps-2021.html, accessed November 25, 2023.

8 The World Bank, https://data.worldbank.org/indicator/
NY.GDP.PCAP.CD, accessed November 25, 2023.

9 "OECD Under Pressure: The Squeezed Middle Class, 2019,"
https://www.oecd.org/els/soc/OECD-middle-class-2019-main-
findings.pdf, accessed November 25, 2023.

10 "OECD Income (IDD) and Wealth (WDD) Distribution
Databases, 2020 or latest," https://www.oecd.org/social/income-
distribution-database.htm, accessed November 22, 2023. On the
Gini Index 0–1 scale, "0" indicates perfect income equality and
"1" indicates perfect inequality.

11 "Poverty in the United States: 2021, United States Census
Bureau," https://www.census.gov/content/dam/Census/library/
publications/2022/demo/p60-277.pdf, accessed November 25,
2023.

12 Human development reports, https://hdr.undp.org/data-center/human-development-index#/indicies/HDI, accessed November 25, 2023.

13 The World Bank, https://data.worldbank.org/indicator/NY.GDP.MKTP.CD?locations=US, accessed November 25, 2023.

14 FRED, "Shares of gross domestic product: Personal consumption expenditures," https://fred.stlouisfed.org/series/DPCERE1Q156NBEA, accessed November 25, 2023.

15 The World Bank, https://data.worldbank.org/indicator/NE.EXP.GNFS.ZS, https://data.worldbank.org/indicator/NE.IMP.GNFS.ZS, accessed November 25, 2023.

16 OECD, "FDI in figures, April 2023," https://www.oecd.org/daf/inv/investment-policy/FDI-in-Figures-April-2023.pdf, accessed November 25, 2023.

17 Observatory of Economic Complexity (OEC), https://oec.world/en/rankings/eci/hs6/hs96?tab=ranking, accessed November 25, 2023.

18 National Science Board, National Science Foundation, "The State of US Science and Engineering 2022," https://ncses.nsf.gov/pubs/nsb20221/executive-summary, accessed November 25, 2023.

19 OECD, "General government debt (2023)," https://www.oecd-ilibrary.org/governance/general-government-debt/indicator/english_a0528cc2-en, accessed November 25, 2023.

20 "IMF Determines New Currency Amounts for the SDR Valuation Basket," July 29, 2022, https://www.imf.org/en/News/Articles/2022/07/29/pr22281-press-release-imf-determines-new-currency-amounts-for-the-sdr-valuation-basket, accessed November 25, 2023.

21 OECD, "General government deficit, 2023," https://www.oecd-ilibrary.org/governance/general-government-deficit/indicator/english_77079edb-en, accessed November 25, 2023.

22 Congressional Budget Office, 2022, https://www.cbo.gov/system/files/2023-03/58888-Budget-Infographic.pdf, accessed November 25, 2023.

23 Ibid.

24 National Archives, "Vietnam War US Military Fatal Casualty Statistics," https://www.archives.gov/research/military/vietnam-war/casualty-statistics, accessed November 25, 2023; Alan Rohn: "Vietnam War Casualties," (2012), https://thevietnamwar.info/vietnam-war-casualties/, accessed November 25, 2023.

25 Such as the Better Life Index (OECD), the Human Development Index (UN), the Inclusive Development Index (World

Economic Forum), the Sustainable Development Goals Index (UN), and the World Happiness Index (UN).

26   Plato, *Gorgias*, 492d, 500c; *Republic*, 352d. http://www.perseus.tufts.edu/hopper/text?doc=Perseus%3Atext%3A1999.01.0178%3Atext%3DGorg.%3Asection%3D492d, accessed January 14, 2024.

27   For the concept of good life and unity of order, see János Csák, *Social Futuring: A Normative Framework*, Working Paper Series No.2/2018, Social Futuring Center, Corvinus University of Budapest, http://socialfuturing.com/storage/uploads/Publications/English/SFC_WP2_Csak.pdf, accessed November 26, 2023.

28   Future Potentials Observatory (FPO), Moholy-Nagy University of Art and Design, https://mome.hu/en/future-potentials-observatory, accessed March 23, 2024.

29   Zoltán Oszkár Szántó, Petra Aczél, Pál Bóday, Péter Harsányi, Future Potential Index | 2022 Concept, Measurements and Results, https://api.mome.hu/uploads/Future_Potential_Index_PPT_5ee60aa904.pdf, accessed March 23, 2024.

NOTES TO CHAPTER FOUR

1   Friedman, *The Storm Before the Calm*, 70.

2   Ibid., 71.

3   The Declaration of Independence of the People of the United States, July 4, 1776, https://www.archives.gov/founding-docs/declaration-transcript, accessed January 15, 2024.

4   The United States Constitution, 1787. https://constitution.congress.gov/constitution/, accessed January 15, 2024.

5   Thomas Jefferson. First Inaugural Address. March 4, 1801. https://founders.archives.gov/documents/Jefferson/01-33-02-0116-0004, accessed January 14, 2024.

6   The United States Constitution, 1787. https://constitution.congress.gov/constitution/, accessed January 15, 2024.

7   "Thomas Jefferson's 'Original Rough Draught' of the Declaration of Independence," in *The Papers of Thomas Jefferson*, Vol. 1, 1760–1776, ed. Julian P. Boyd (Princeton, NJ: Princeton University Press, 1950), 243–47.

8   Thomas Jefferson Foundation, "Jefferson and American Indians," https://www.monticello.org/thomas-jefferson/louisiana-lewis-clark/origins-of-the-expedition/jefferson-and-american-indians/, accessed November 26, 2023.

9   Samuel Johnson, "Taxation No Tyranny. An Answer to the Resolutions and Address of the American Congress, 1775" (London: Printed for T. Cadell, in the Strand, MDCCXXV), 89.

10   Thomas Jefferson, "Notes on the State of Virginia, 1743–1826" (147, 173), https://docsouth.unc.edu/southlit/jefferson/jefferson.html, accessed November 26, 2023.

11   Daniel Boorstin, *The Americans: The National Experience* (New York: Vintage Books, 1965), 200.

12   Quoted from William M. Wiecek, "Somerset: Lord Mansfield and the Legitimacy of Slavery in the Anglo-American World," *The University of Chicago Law Review* (1974), 87–88, https://chicagounbound.uchicago.edu/cgi/viewcontent.cgi?article=3831&context=uclrev, accessed November 26, 2023.

13   Tocqueville, 336.

14   Tocqueville, 354–55.

15   Goldman, *After Nationalism*, 27.

16   Ibid., 87–88.

17   Abraham Lincoln, "'House Divided' Speech," http://www.abrahamlincolnonline.org/lincoln/speeches/house.htm, accessed November 26, 2023.

18   "The Lincoln-Douglas debate. Seventh Debate, Alton, Illinois, October 15, 1855," https://www.nps.gov/liho/learn/historyculture/debate7.htm, accessed November 26, 2023.

19   Quoted from Goldman, *After Nationalism*, 56.

20   Order of Argument; 12/1953; Case File for *Brown et al. v. Board of Education of Topeka et al.*; Appellate Jurisdiction Case Files, 1792 - 2010; Records of the Supreme Court of the United States, Record Group 267; National Archives Building, Washington, DC, https://www.docsteach.org/documents/document/order-of-argument, accessed January 14, 2024

21   Martin Luther King, "I have a dream, 28 August 1963," http://news.bbc.co.uk/2/hi/americas/3170387.stm, accessed November 26, 2023.

22   Quoted from Goldman, *After Nationalism*, 90.

23   "Declarations and Resolutions of the First Continental Congress, October 14, 1774," https://avalon.law.yale.edu/18th_century/resolves.asp, accessed November 26, 2023.

24   *Library of Congress Journals of the Continental Congress, 1774–1789*, Volume XXXII (Washington: US Government Printing Office, 1936), 318. https://www.loc.gov/resource/llscdam.lljc032/?sp=344&st=pdf&r=-0.397%2C-0.084%2C1.794%2C1.794%2C0&pdfPage=328, accessed January 14, 2024.

25   From "George Washington to the United States Senate and House of Representatives, 30 January 1794," https://founders.archives.gov/documents/Washington/05-15-02-0122, accessed November 26, 2023.

26 Woodrow Borah, "The Historical Demography of Aboriginal and Colonial America: An Attempt at Perspective," in William M. Denevan, ed., *The Native Population of the Americas in 1492* (Madison, WI: University of Wisconsin Press, 1976), 13–34.

27 "The American Indian and Alaska Native Population: 2010 Census Briefs, January 2012," https://www.census.gov/content/dam/Census/library/publications/2012/dec/c2010br-10.pdf, accessed November 26, 2023; Sandra L. Colby, Jennifer M. Ortman, "Projections of the Size and Composition of the US Population: 2014–2060, 2015," https://www.census.gov/content/dam/Census/library/publications/2015/demo/p25-1143.pdf, accessed November 26, 2023.

28 Tocqueville, 404.

29 These included the 1675–1678 campaign of Chief Metacomet of the Wampanoag, known as King Philip, against the colony of Plymouth, the war of the Tuscarora in 1712, and the war of the Chief of Pontiac Odawa in 1763, as well as, later, the wars of the Onondaga, the Cayuga, the Oneida, the Seneca, the battles of the Shawnee chief Tecumseh and his tribal federation, or the Seminoles of Osceola.

30 Zachary Brown, "The Rhetoric and Practice of Scalping," *Journal of the American Revolution*, September 1, 2016, https://allthingsliberty.com/2016/09/rhetoric-practice-scalping/#_ednref16, accessed November 26, 2023.

31 Henry J. Young, "A Note on Scalp Bounties in Pennsylvania," *Pennsylvania History: A Journal of Mid-Atlantic Studies* 24, no. 3 (Penn State University Press, 1957), 209, http://www.jstor.org/stable/27769743, accessed November 26, 2023.

32 Samuel G. Drake, *A Particular History of the Five Years French and Indian War in New England and Parts Adjacent, from Its Declaration by the King of France, March 15, 1744, to the Treaty with the Eastern Indians, Oct. 16, 1749, Sometimes Called Governor Shirley's War: With a Memoir of Major-General Shirley, Accompanied by His Portrait and Other Engravings* (Albany: Joel Munsell Publishing), 134, https://books.google.hu/books?id=AX-IvAAAAYAAJ&printsec=frontcover&hl=hu&source=gbs_ge_summary_r&cad=0#v=onepage&q&f=false, accessed November 26, 2023.

33 Grahame Allen, "Inflation: the value of the pound 1750–2011," House of Commons Library, 29 May 2012, https://researchbriefings.files.parliament.uk/documents/RP12-31/RP12-31.pdf, accessed November 26, 2023.

34 "A Declaration and Remonstrance Of the distressed and

bleeding Frontier Inhabitants Of the Province of Pennsylvania, Presented by them to the Honourable the Governor and Assembly of the Province, Shewing the Causes Of their late Discontent and Uneasiness and the Grievances Under which they have laboured, and which they humbly pray to have redress'd," in John R. Dunbar, ed., *The Paxton Papers* (The Hague, 1957), 99–110. See also Pennsylvania Assembly Committee: Report, 21 February 1764, https://founders.archives.gov/documents/ Franklin/01-11-02-0017#BNFN-01-11-02-0017-fn-0002, accessed January 14, 2024.

35 Peter d'Errico, "Jeffrey Amherst and Smallpox Blankets, (2020)," https://people.umass.edu/derrico/amherst/lord_jeff.html, accessed November 26, 2023; Elizabeth A. Fenn, *Pox Americana: The Great Smallpox Epidemic of 1775-82* (New York: Hill and Wang, 2001), https://people.umass.edu/derrico/amherst/fenn. html, accessed November 26, 2023.

36 Paul Corcoran, "John Locke on the Possession of Land: Native Title vs. the 'Principle' of Vacuum domicilium," https:// digital.library.adelaide.edu.au/dspace/bitstream/2440/44958/1/ hdl_44958.pdf, accessed November 26, 2023.

37 Neal Salisbury, *Manitou and Providence: Indians, Europeans, and the Making of New England, 1500–1643* (New York and Oxford: Oxford University Press, 1982), 176.

38 "James Monroe's First State of the Union Address, 12 December 1817," https://en.wikisource.org/wiki/James_Monroe %27s_First_State_of_the_Union_Address, accessed November 26, 2023.

39 President James Monroe, in an 1825 message to Congress, Messages and Papers of the Presidents, in *Native American Voices: A History and Anthology,* ed. Steven Mintz (St. James, NY: Brandywine, 1995), 111–12, http://www.columbia. edu/~lmg21/ash3002y/usindpol.html, accessed November 26, 2023.

40 Andrew Jackson, Letter to the Creek Indians, March 23, 1829, https://www.presidency.ucsb.edu/documents/letter-the-creek-indians, accessed January 14, 2024

41 "Andrew Jackson's Message to Congress, 'On Indian Removal,'" December 6, 1830, https://www.nps.gov/museum/ tmc/MANZ/handouts/Andrew_Jackson_Annual_Message.pdf, accessed November 26, 2023.

42 Tocqueville, 334–35.

43 *Sand Creek Massacre,* US National Park Service, https:// www.nps.gov/sand/learn/historyculture/index.htm, accessed

November 26, 2023

44   *Life of Silas Soule,* https://www.nps.gov/sand/learn/historyculture/the-life-of-silas-soule.htm, https://www.nps.gov/sand/learn/historyculture/joseph-cramer-biography.htm, accessed November 26, 2023.

45   *Report of the Secretary Of War, Being Part Of The Message And Documents Communicated To The Two Houses Of Congress, Beginning Of The Second Session Of The Forty-Fifth Congress, Volume I* (Washington: Government Printing Office, 1877), 630; Joseph, "An Indian's View of Indian Affairs," *The North American Review,* http://www.americanyawp.com/reader/17-conquering-the-west/chief-joseph-on-indian-affairs-1877-1879/, accessed November 26, 2023.

46   Friedman, *The Storm Before the Calm,* 74.

NOTES TO CHAPTER FIVE

1   Gunnar Myrdal, *An American Dilemma: The Negro Problem and Modern Democracy* (New York and London: Harper and Brothers, 1944), xlviii.

2   Shortly after Lincoln's first election as president in 1861, his third son, Willie, died in 1862 at the age of 12. In his pain over his son's death, he suffered what today we would diagnose as clinical depression and, according to his wife, was "getting closer and closer to God." Lincoln had a total of four sons, and the second, Eddie, died in 1852 at the age of just four.

3   Abraham Lincoln, "Address Before the Young Men's Lyceum of Springfield, Illinois, January 27, 1837," https://digital.lib.niu.edu/islandora/object/niu-lincoln%3A35565, accessed November 26, 2023.

4   Abraham Lincoln, "Letter to Joshua F. Speed, August 24, 1855," https://www.nps.gov/liho/learn/historyculture/knownothingparty.htm, accessed November 26, 2023.

5   Abraham Lincoln, "Annual Message to Congress, Washington, D. C. December 1, 1862," http://www.abrahamlincolnonline.org/lincoln/speeches/congress.htm, accessed November 26, 2023.

6   Abraham Lincoln, "Proclamation Appointing a National Fast Day, Washington, D. C., March 30, 1863," http://www.abrahamlincolnonline.org/lincoln/speeches/fast.htm, accessed November 26, 2023.

7   Abraham Lincoln, "Second Inaugural Address, Washington, D. C., March 4, 1865," http://144.208.79.222/~abraha21/alo/lincoln/speeches/inaug2.htm, accessed November 26, 2023.

8   *Thucydides, Translated into English with Introduction,*

Marginal Analysis, Notes, and Indices by B. Jowett (Oxford: Clarendon Press, 1881), 399–402.

9   Tocqueville, 154.

10   Paul Horgan, *Great River: The Rio Grande in North American History*, 2 vols. (New York: Rinehart and Company, 1954).

11   Amy Greenberg, *Manifest Destiny and American Territorial Expansion: A Brief History With Documents* (Boston and New York: Bedford, and St. Martin's: Macmillan Learning, 2018).

12   Abraham Lincoln, "Second Inaugural Address, Washington, D. C., March 4, 1865," http://144.208.79.222/~abraha21/alo/lincoln/speeches/inaug2.htm, accessed November 26, 2023.

13   "Notes on the State of Virginia: Jefferson, Thomas, 1743–1826" (173), https://docsouth.unc.edu/southlit/jefferson/jefferson.html, accessed November 25, 2023.

NOTES TO CHAPTER SIX

1   Paul Johnson, *Intellectuals* (London: Phoenix, an imprint of Orion Books Ltd., 1996 [1988]), 1–2.

2   Saul D. Alinsky, *Reveille for Radicals* (Chicago: University of Chicago Press, 1946), 11.

3   Saul D. Alinsky, *Rules for Radicals: A Practical Primer for Realistic Radicals* (New York: Vintage Books, 1972), 116.

4   Gerald Astor, "The 'Apostle' and The 'Fool,'" *Look* (June 25, 1968), 34.

5   Patrick Anderson, "Making Trouble is Alinsky's Business," *The New York Times Magazine* (October 9, 1966), 102.

6   Quoted from Hillary D. Rodham (Clinton), "There is only the Fight..., An Analysis of the Alinsky Model," BA thesis, Special Honors Program, Wellesley College, Wellesley, MA (May 2, 1969), https://www.economicpolicyjournal.com/2013/04/hillary-clintons-1969-thesis-on-saul.html, accessed November 26, 2023. 72: Saul D. Alinsky, "Is There Life After Birth? Speech presented before the Centennial Meeting of the Episcopal Theological School, Cambridge, MA, June 7, 1967," *Anglican Theological Review*, January 1968.

7   Hillary D. Rodham (Clinton), "There is only the Fight..., An Analysis of the Alinsky Model," 74, https://www.economicpolicyjournal.com/2013/04/hillary-clintons-1969-thesis-on-saul.html, accessed November 26, 2023.

8   Herbert Marcuse, "Repressive Tolerance," in Robert Paul Wolff, Barrington Moore, Jr., and Herbert Marcuse, *A Critique of Pure Tolerance* (Boston: Beacon Press, 1969), https://www.marcuse.org/herbert/publications/1960s/1965-repressive-tolerance-1969.

pdf, accessed November 26, 2023.

9   Ibid., 81–83.

10   Ibid., 107.

11   Ibid., 92.

12   Ibid., 95.

13   Ibid., 121.

14   Ibid., 101.

15   Ibid., 197.

16   Ibid., 109.

17   Ibid., 116.

18   Ibid., 119–20.

19   Ibid., 100.

20   Ibid., 123.

21   Ibid., 101.

22   Ibid., 110.

23   Ronald Reagan, "Inaugural Address (Public Ceremony), January 5, 1967," https://www.reaganlibrary.gov/archives/speech/january-5-1967-inaugural-address-public-ceremony, accessed December 1, 2023.

24   See Roger Kimball, "The Right Targets," *The New Criterion* Volume 40 Number 5 (January 2022), https://newcriterion.com/issues/2022/1/the-right-targets, accessed November 26, 2023.

25   The Heritage Foundation, "Mission," https://www.heritage.org/about-heritage/mission, accessed November 26, 2023.

26   Cato Institute, "The vision of the Cato Institute," https://www.cato.org/about, accessed November 26, 2023.

27   American Enterprise Institute, "AEI's Organization and Purpose," https://www.aei.org/about/aeis-organization-and-purposes/, accessed November 26, 2023.

28   Ethics and Public Policy Center, "Economics and Ethics Program," https://eppc.org/program/economics-and-ethics/, accessed November 26, 2023.

29   Acton Institute, "Our Mission & Core Principles," https://www.acton.org/about/mission, accessed November 26, 2023.

30   Brookings Institution, "Annual Report, 2021," https://annualreport.brookings.edu/co-chairs-letter-presidents-letter/, accessed November 26, 2023.

31   Center for Economic Security and Opportunity, https://www.brookings.edu/centers/center-for-economic-security-and-opportunity/about-the-center/, accessed December 1, 2023.

32   Rakesh Kochhar and Stella Sechopoulos, "How the American middle class has changed in the past five decades" (April

20, 2022), https://www.pewresearch.org/short-reads/2022/04/20/how-the-american-middle-class-has-changed-in-the-past-five-decades/, accessed December 1, 2023.

33 Homi Kharas, "Disquiet in the world's middle class" (November 21, 2023), https://www.brookings.edu/articles/disquiet-in-the-worlds-middle-class/, accessed December 1, 2023.

34 National Center for Drug Abuse Statistics (NCDAS), "Opioid Epidemic: Addiction Statistics," https://drugabusestatistics.org/opioid-epidemic/. NCDAS, "Alcohol Abuse Statistics," https://drugabusestatistics.org/alcohol-abuse-statistics/. Tom Cotton, "Crime, Policing, And Public Safety In America," https://www.manhattan-institute.org/senator-tom-cotton-crime-policing-and-public-safety; Holly Hedegaard—Sally C. Curtin—Margaret Warner, "Suicide Mortality in the United States, 1999–2019," US Department of Health and Human Services, https://www.cdc.gov/nchs/data/databriefs/db398-H.pdf, all accessed February 22, 2022.

35 Charles Murray, *Coming Apart: The State of White America, 1960–2010* (New York: Crown Forum, 2012).

36 David Goodhart, *Head, Hand, Heart: The Struggle for Dignity and Status in the 21st Century* (London: Penguin, 2019).

37 Plato, *Apology*, 30b, http://www.perseus.tufts.edu/hopper/text?doc=Perseus%3Atext%3A1999.01.0170%3Atext%3DApol.%3Asection%3D30b, accessed January 17, 2024.

38 John Haldane, *Practical Philosophy: Ethics, Society and Culture* (Exeter: Imprint Academic, 2009), 171.

39 For psychological studies and experiments on attachment, see Jude Cassidy and Phillip R. Shaver, eds, *Handbook of Attachment, Theory, Research, and Clinical Applications*, Third Edition (New York: The Guilford Press, 2016); John Bowlby, *Attachment and Loss: Attachment* (New York: Basic Books, 1999 [1969]).

40 James Heckman, "Family Matters," Center for Economics of Human Development, The University of Chicago, https://heckmanequation.org/resource/family-matters/, accessed December 1, 2023; James J. Heckman and Stefano Mosso, "The Economics of Human Development and Social Mobility" (Department of Economics, University of Chicago, May 20, 2014), https://heckmanequation.org/assets/2017/01/Econ-of-Hum-Dev-and-Soc-Mob_2014-05-20a_akc.pdf, accessed December 1, 2023.

41 George Weigel, "American Democracy's Moral and Cultural Foundations," November 11, 2020, Ethics and Public Policy Center, https://eppc.org/publication/american-democracys-moral-and-cultural-foundations/, accessed December 1, 2023.

42 "Pierce v. Society of Sisters," Supreme Court of the United States, 1925, https://www.law.cornell.edu/supremecourt/text/268/510; Berkley Center for Religion, Peace, and World Affairs, Georgetown University, https://berkleycenter.georgetown.edu/cases/pierce-v-society-of-sisters, accessed December 1, 2023.

43 Acton Institute, "Our Mission & Core Principles," https://www.acton.org/about/mission, accessed February 22, 2022.

44 For child and family benefits, I rely on: Office of Management and Budget, *Budget of the United States Government, Fiscal Year 2022* (Washington, DC: US Government Printing Office, 2021); Urban Institute studies: Heather Hahn—Cary Lou—Julia B. Isaacs—Eleanor Lauderback—Hannah Daly—C. Eugene Steuerle, *Kids' Share 2023: Report on Federal Expenditures on Children through 2022 and Future Projections*, November 9, 2023, https://www.urban.org/research/publication/kids-share-2023, accessed December 1, 2023.

NOTES TO EPILOGUE

1 George Washington, *Farewell Address, 19th September 1796*, https://founders.archives.gov/documents/Washington/05-20-02-0440-0002, accessed January 17, 2024.

2 Tocqueville, 361–62.

3 Ibid., 373.

4 Ibid., 382.

5 Ibid., 383.

6 Ibid., 385.

7 John Courtney Murray, S. J., *We Hold These Truths: Catholic Reflections on the American Proposition* (New York: Sheed and Ward, 1960).

8 John Winthrop, *A Model of Christian Charity* [1630] (Boston: Collections of the Massachusetts Historical Society, 1838), https://history.hanover.edu/texts/winthmod.html, accessed November 25, 2023.

9 Leo Strauss, *Natural Right and History* (Chicago: University of Chicago Press, 1953), 74.

10 Alasdair Macintyre, *After Virtue, A Study in Moral Theory*, third edition (Notre Dame, IN: University of Notre Dame Press, 2007), 219.

11 Ibid., xvi.

ABOUT THE AUTHOR

JÁNOS ZOLTÁN CSÁK, economist-sociologist, honorary professor, Ambassador of Hungary to the United Kingdom from 2011 to 2014, Minister of Culture and Innovation since 2022. He focuses on strategy and finance, organizational capabilities, and management development. During his career he has worked as Chairman, CEO, and board member in a number of companies in the energy, telecommunications, banking, and academic sectors in Europe, North America, and Australia. In 2009–2010, he was a visiting scholar at The Heritage Foundation in Washington, DC and at the Acton Institute in Grand Rapids, MI. He is the author of several essays and studies and a recipient of the Commander's Cross of the Hungarian Order of Merit.